The Vinyl Dialogues

Stories behind memorable albums
of the 1970s
as told by the artists

by Mike Morsch

i

**For my mom and dad,
who had a great vinyl collection.**

Cover design by Ron Dacanay.
Editing by Frank D. Quattrone and Ruth Littner and
Ann Stolinsky of Gemini Wordsmiths.

ISBN: 978-1-62249-207-7
Library of Congress Control Number: 2014908973

Published by
Biblio Publishing
BiblioPublishing.com

Contents

Everything old is new again

Introduction
Mike Morsch

When I was a kid growing up in central Illinois, my folks had a record collection that consisted of popular music from the late 1950s to the mid-1960s. I played those vinyl albums — Elvis, The Beach Boys, The Beatles, The Association, and many more — so much that I wore them out.

By the time the 1970s rolled around and I was in high school, I was more into eight-track tapes, cassettes, big bushy sideburns, and bell-bottomed pants. ("Seventies suave" indeed.)

And I still didn't have my own record collection.

More than 35 years later I decided to change that. For Christmas 2013, my wife got me a turntable because I told her I was going to start a record collection. The premise was that I wanted to hear the early work of some of my favorite artists, and my thinking was that listening on vinyl would offer me the purest form of the music.

This hobby developed into a labor of love for me.

I spent time researching a band and its music, chose an album I thought I'd like to have in my collection, and went to the record store in search of the album. Fortunately, there are still a few record stores around my part of southeastern Pennsylvania, and there's a certain nostalgic charm about going into one and searching through the albums.

The Vinyl Dialogues

The first album I coveted was *Abandoned Luncheonette* by Daryl Hall & John Oates. I suspect that since I didn't grow up on the East Coast, I was unaware of the early Hall & Oates stuff because they didn't have country-wide recognition back then. So I had never really heard the entire album as a single body of work.

Anyone who's a treasure hunter of sorts — be it at an antique store, garage sale, or baseball card show — knows that feeling of elation upon actually finding that one thing you've been searching for, and that's what happened to me with *Abandoned Luncheonette*.

It was sitting in plain sight in one of the bins, and I spotted it instantly as I walked through the door of The Vinyl Closet, a quaint little record shop on Main Street in North Wales, Pennsylvania, owned by Jason McFarland.

I bought the album for $1; it was in fabulous shape. Naturally, I rushed home to play it on my new turntable and I was immediately transported back to the early 1970s in my mind. I was listening to the origins of what is now known as "Philly soul" or the "sound of Philadelphia," and it was, and is, a really cool vibe.

As I was examining the cover art, I flipped the record over and read the information on the back. There, at the bottom in small print, were the words, "1973 Atlantic Recording Corporation."

Hey, I thought to myself, *2013 is the 40th anniversary of the release of that album. I wonder if Daryl and John would want talk about it?*

I emailed Jonathan Wolfson, the manager for Hall & Oates, and he responded the same day saying he thought that a story about the 40th anniversary of *Abandoned Luncheonette* was "a great idea" and that he would make Daryl and John available for interviews.

Within a week I had both artists on the phone in separate interviews for a story that I was writing for my news organization at the time, Montgomery Media, in

2

Fort Washington, Pennsylvania. Both Daryl and John shared their recollections about making *Abandoned Luncheonette* and the story of how they got the now-famous photographs that grace the front and back covers of the album, those of a forgotten diner that once rested on the outskirts of Pottstown, Pennsylvania, just off Route 724, not far from where I live.

The Hall & Oates interviews were so fun and informative that I began to wonder if others artists from the 1970s would talk about their experiences and recollections of making specific albums.

And that's how the idea for this book was born. All I needed to do was execute.

I asked other favorite musicians; they answered "Yes!"

And that's what you'll read about here — those memorable stories from the artists who made such brilliant music in the 1970s — in *The Vinyl Dialogues*.

It all started because I found an album at a local record store for a dollar, took it home and listened to it, and discovered the early sounds of Philly soul.

And everything old is new again.

— Mike Morsch

We were lazy slobs; we didn't work at it

Burrito Deluxe
The Flying Burrito Brothers

*T*t had all started out so well for The Flying Burrito Brothers. And those good feelings continued into the early recording of their second album, *Burrito Deluxe*. But before the completion of *Burrito Deluxe*, The Flying Burrito Brothers were starting to lose it. One of the reasons was that guitarist Gram Parsons was having trouble staying focused on the music he was creating, because he was infatuated with Keith Richards.

The group's first album, *The Gilded Palace of Sin*, released in 1969, had helped cement the reputations of Parsons and Chris Hillman — two of the original members of The Byrds — as innovators in what was then the early stages of a new genre, "country rock."

The original Flying Burrito Brothers — Parsons, mandolin player Hillman, bassist Chris Ethridge, and pedal steel guitarist "Sneaky" Pete Kleinow — was founded in 1968. After *The Gilded Palace of Sin* was released, the band hired another ex-Byrds member, drummer Michael Clarke, and lost Ethridge, who was replaced by Bernie Leadon. In 1970, the reshuffled lineup set out to record its second album, *Burrito Deluxe*. In the two and-a-half years since Parsons and Hillman had left the Byrds, and up to the recording of *Burrito Deluxe*, almost everything had been going smoothly between the

5

two collaborators. Then Gram Parsons met Keith Richards.

"Gram was starting to lose interest and was hanging out a lot with Keith," said Hillman. "That's how we ended up with the song 'Wild Horses.'" Written by Richards and Mick Jagger of the Rolling Stones, "Wild Horses" was the 11th and final song cut by the Burritos for *Burrito Deluxe*.

Chris Hillman, left, and Bill Bryson, members of the Desert Rose Band, appeared at the Sellersville Theater 1894 in Sellersville, PA, in April 2013. Hillman is an original member of The Byrds and The Flying Burrito Brothers and was a frequent collaborator of the late Gram Parsons.
(Photo by Mike Morsch)

"With all due respect for Mick and Keith, I hated that song," said Hillman. "They did it quite well, but Gram was caterwauling on that song and it drove me up the wall."

6

Hillman described Parsons' influence on Jagger and Richards as "sort of a Johnny Appleseed thing," turning the two rockers on to country music.

"And they came up with 'Wild Horses' in that sort of groove," said Hillman. "They said, 'Hey, you guys cut it,' meaning we could cut it before they did, which was an honor."

Time has softened Hillman's feelings about the song. But in 1970, that wasn't the case.

"I retract my original statement," said Hillman. "What Mick and Keith had done with 'Wild Horses,' it was well put in the lyric. 'Wild horses couldn't drag me away' — that's a great poetic line with great imagery. But as a player of that groove, and with Gram singing it at that particular time, it wasn't resonating the way Mick Jagger sang it."

In addition to the Jagger-Richards tune "Wild Horses," the Parsons-Hillman-Leadon-penned "Cody, Cody" became the second cut on Side Two of the album. And once again, Hillman didn't much like the song, but for a completely different reason.

"I can't stand it, and I wrote it," said Hillman. "It's not a bad song, but it's a little strange in the lyric. However, we really didn't nail it. I gotta tell you something — and I don't tell this to many people," said Hillman. "I came from the Byrds, where we learned how to play and we went from covering Bob Dylan songs to doing songs like 'Eight Miles High' [written for the Byrds by band members Gene Clark, Roger McGuinn, and David Crosby]. We were really a solid band and very sophisticated.

"But the Burritos . . . we were lazy slobs," he said. "We didn't work at it. We had the material, but the execution was a little flawed. I hold myself responsible, although it doesn't matter now. But I should have been

7

cracking the whip on those guys. I knew better, but I just sort of let things go . . . that lackadaisical approach. In some ways it worked and in some ways it didn't. 'Cody, Cody' is an example of that."

The cut "High Fashion Queen," a song on the same album, is another instance of where the group was not able to nail it, according to Hillman. But unlike "Cody, Cody," Hillman got another swing at that one, albeit nearly 30 years later.

"About three years after we cut 'High Fashion Queen,' I said, 'Someday I want to record that properly.' It's supposed to be a country shuffle and not so frantic," he said.

In 1999, Hillman finally got the chance. Songwriter and performer Emmylou Harris produced an album titled, *Return of the Grievous Angel: A Tribute to Gram Parsons*, and on that record Hillman asked musician, songwriter, and author Steve Earle to cut a version of "High Fashion Queen."

"So Steve and I sang it in a straight country shuffle, the way it should have been cut the first time. Once in a while I get a chance to redo something that I didn't quite nail the first time, and 'High Fashion Queen' is a great song. That was when Gram and I were writing on a level of the stuff on the first album [*The Gilded Palace of Sin*]."

But loss of focus continued to plague *Burrito Deluxe*. And Hillman was losing Parsons.

"Gram had talent. But it's one thing to have talent; it's another thing to have the work ethic to make that happen," said Hillman. "And he wasted it, wasted it, wasted it. We were losing him at that point in time. Gram was an ambitious kid, and he was a dear, dear friend, but he wasn't a loyal guy. We were brothers, but we became Cain and Abel. Seriously, that's the way to describe it."

8

Instead of putting in the studio work needed to complete *Burrito Deluxe*, Parsons continued to spend time with Richards and the Stones. In addition, Parsons was missing paying gigs, instead choosing to hang out at Stones' recording sessions. It was well documented that Parsons had fallen into serious drug and alcohol abuse.

"I had to literally go into the session and get him because we had a gig to do," said Hillman. "That's when Jagger came over — Mick was the consummate professional — and said, 'You have a show to do . . . and we're working here.' That's a key line: 'We're working here,' meaning 'You're in the way.' That's a great line. There was no love lost between Mick and Gram, I'll tell you."

Eventually, the Burritos had to fire Parsons.

"It's all in print, where he'd show up out of his mind, inebriated, you name it, and show up to a show," said Hillman. "And the rest of us were there to work. Bernie [Leadon] is a professional musician; he's an on-the-money great player. And Sneaky [Pete Kleinow] is a professional. And then here comes Gram, barely able to walk, coming into the show. It eventually got to where we had to let him go."

Parsons died of a drug overdose on September 19, 1973 — at age 26 — in a hotel in Joshua Tree, California, less than three years after *Burrito Deluxe* was released.

The album cover of *Burrito Deluxe* shows the band members dressed in what Hillman called "radioactive lab jumpsuits" and plastic gloves in the upper left corner of the cover, but the dominant art on the page is a photo of two big burritos.

"The cover was Gram's idea," said Hillman. "He had the greatest sense of humor, but a little off. But I can't even make something up now as to why we did it that way."

The transition from the Byrds to the Flying Burrito Brothers wasn't the first step toward country rock for Parsons and Hillman.

"Gram really was responsible for taking songs from another genre — not that he was the first one, though," said Hillman. "You can go back to Ray Charles and Buck Owens songs in the early 1960s, but Gram made it work."

As an example, Hillman offered up the Burritos' versions of two songs — "Do Right Woman" and "Dark End of the Street" — both written by Chips Moman and Dan Penn, and both of which appeared on *The Gilded Palace of Sin.*

"Gram would say, 'Let's cut "Do Right Woman." And I'd say, 'OK, I love the song, but it's a woman's song.' And he'd say, 'We'll make it work.' And we did. We took Aretha Franklin's 'Do Right Woman' and made it work," said Hillman.

The original Flying Burrito Brothers were together only a few years and would record only two more albums, the eponymous *The Flying Burrito Brothers* in 1971 and *Last of the Red Hot Burritos* in 1972. After Parsons was let go, Rick Roberts joined the band on vocals and rhythm guitar for the third album. After that, Kleinow left the group and became a session musician; Leadon soon followed and helped create the Eagles. Hillman was the last to go, joining Stephen Stills in the band Manassas for a short time. Still, more than 40 years after recording *Burrito Deluxe*, Hillman said it was a memorable experience.

"The music was great. It happened the way it was supposed to happen in an ethereal-spiritual sense," said Hillman. "I got a lot out of it. I wrote some of my best songs with Gram, I really did.

10

"The stuff we did together on the first album —
Sin City — has been covered by four or five major artists.
And Gram was a great guy to work with."

In the 1980s, Hillman formed the Desert Rose
Band and became one of the most successful country
music acts throughout the 1980s and early 1990s. The
band had two No. 1 hits in 1988 — "He's Back and I'm
Blue" and "I Still Believe in You." Although the Desert
Rose Band officially disbanded in the early 1990s,
Hillman still performs with some original members,
including Herb Pedersen, John Jorgenson, and Bill
Bryson.

"My audience now is my age — that's the general
demographic," said Hillman. "The other part that's really
great — and I love this — is that I get young kids coming
to concerts who love The Byrds and the Flying Burrito
Brothers; kids in their 20s — they just love that stuff and
they're playing that kind of music and it's very flattering."

As of 2013, Hillman had been in the music
business for 50 years. He's still having a great time and
Burrito Deluxe was one of those great times that came
along in his life.

"Did we know what we were doing back then? Not
really," said Hillman. "I never thought I'd get paid —
none of us did. It was all about the passion for the music.
I love to play, I'm glad I can still play, and I'm glad
people still want to hear me play.

The smoke shack that produced a '*Sgt. Pepper*'

Cosmo's Factory
Creedence Clearwater Revival

*T*he title of Creedence Clearwater Revival's fifth studio album, *Cosmo's Factory*, evolved from the nickname of one of the band's members, advanced to a small gardener's shack — so full of smoke that not only rehearsing, but breathing, proved difficult — and eventually became what one of its creators called the band's *Sgt. Pepper*.

That's how CCR's original drummer, Doug "Cosmo" Clifford remembers it.

Clifford's nickname predates Creedence Clearwater Revival, which included lead vocalist and lead guitarist John Fogerty, his brother, rhythm guitarist Tom Fogerty, bassist Stu Cook, and drummer Clifford. The four had known each other since junior high school in the late 1950s in California, and had played together as The Blue Velvets since the early 1960s. Cook and Clifford went off to college at San Jose State in the mid-1960s, and it was there that Clifford got the nickname "Cosmo."

"Stu and I lived literally in the 'Animal House.' It was grand but it had really seen better days," said Clifford. "We were supposed to be a fraternity but we were on suspension — double secret probation, whatever — and there was no adult supervision there. So it was a

13

pretty wild place. Of course the students were pigs. Half-eaten burgers in their rooms; just never would clean up after themselves. So we had a roach problem."

As a youngster, Clifford was an amateur entomologist, collecting butterflies and moths. That evolved into an interest in insects like bees, wasps, and termites. By the time college rolled around, Clifford was seen as the closest thing in his "Animal House" to an expert in getting rid of its roach problems.

"There had been an ant problem long before I was there. They had pest control come out and nobody could get rid of the ants," said Clifford. "So I said I could get rid of the ants and I could get rid of the roaches, but I needed help. You guys have to clean up — and I mean really clean up — and continue to keep things clean or otherwise I'm not going to do it."

Pest control in the mid-1960s consisted of what Clifford called "lethal poisons that were like weapons of mass destruction." So Clifford made "little food bombs" of poison for the roaches and ants, and that did the trick.

"So finally after two or three weeks of working hard on doing that, the house was pest-free, except for a couple of the guys I wanted to poison, but that's another story," said Clifford.

A few weeks later, Cook and Clifford were at a party, drinking cheap wine — because that's all they could afford, according to Clifford. His reputation as a pest control expert had followed him to the party. He was known by the guys in the frat house as "Clifford C. Clifford" — an inside joke. Someone at the party asked what the "C" stood for.

"And before I could respond — this was like in 1965 maybe — someone said, 'It stands for Cosmo because he's cosmic; he's a man of nature.' That's the story," said Clifford.

Flash ahead a few years to the second half of the 1960s. Creedence Clearwater Revival had yet to release its first album. The band used to practice in Tom Fogerty's garage.

"We were literally a garage band. To this day, I consider us the best garage band in the world. That's how I have perceived us all these years. We worked hard to do that," said Clifford. But the neighbors complained about the noise coming from the garage and the police were called on several occasions. The last time law enforcement arrived, they told the band members they had better find another place to practice, or they'd have their equipment impounded and risk arrest.

Just at that time, Clifford and his wife were renting a house and had just had their first child. Behind the house was a small gardener's shack, and Clifford suggested that the band rehearse there.

"I mean it was a ridiculously small place. It had a glass window that there was no way to open. I had an old rug rolled up in there and I cut it up and tacked it onto the walls to absorb a little of the sound. I would say maybe it was 10 feet x 6 feet," said Clifford.

At the time, everybody in the band except Clifford smoked cigarettes while they were practicing.

"We were working on a song and we'd been there like an hour and it would be hard enough being in there for an hour sitting and doing nothing but playing drums; my heart rate was up, my breathing was up. These guys were just pounding the smokes," said Clifford.

"I had finally had enough. I said, 'I can't stand it anymore!' I got up and threw my sticks down, pushed open the door and started breathing fresh air. The guys said, 'What's the problem?' I said, 'You guys are smoking me out of here. I can't breathe. I don't know how you do it.' And Tom Fogerty said, 'Well, it's better than working in a factory somewhere.' So the seed was planted," said Clifford.

The next day, Clifford took a piece of 1 x 4 x 15-inch wood and painted "The Factory" on it, and nailed it onto the door of the shack. And that became the original "Cosmo's Factory."

Once the band became successful, it needed a newer and bigger facility in which to make music.

"So we went into the industrial section of Berkeley, California and picked an old wooden structure with multiple stories. When we leased that building, then that became 'Cosmo's Factory,'" said Clifford.

With each album, CCR's stock continued to grow and John Fogerty asserted himself even more. He had become the band's principal songwriter and leader.

"John was under a lot of stress because, unfortunately, he had undertaken the duties of being the manager for the band. He's a brilliant talent, but he didn't know anything about business," said Clifford.

"John thought he could do this. But he let that whole side consume him. And we were left out in the cold on that. We never knew what was going on. When we would call him on it, he would get very angry and it was a nightmare."

And John Fogerty had shut his older brother Tom out of doing anything creative with the band.

According to Clifford, Tom Fogerty was a gentle guy who had devised the original concept of the band. Tom was in a band called Spider Webb and the Insects at the same time as John Fogerty, Cook, and Clifford were performing as The Blue Velvets, an instrumental trio.

16

Tom Fogerty's band eventually went belly up —
the members said they would rather work on their cars
than learn the songs. So Tom approached The Blue
Velvets to work out some sort of arrangement. They
agreed to join forces to record and perform under the
name Tommy Fogerty and The Blue Velvets.

"Tom enlisted us to back him up and we were
terrible. But he stuck with us and we eventually got better.
We worked at it and worked at it. He was generous and
treated us with patience and dignity. That was his
strength. We owed him a lot. And we were lucky that he
brought us on or it never would have happened for us,"
said Clifford.

When John Fogerty took over the lead vocals for
CCR, Tom gave them up, but expected to sing a song or
two, Clifford said. Only one of Tom's songs, "Walking on
the Water," was ever recorded.

"The Beatles sang different songs and it wasn't just
one singer. So when we had success, John told Tom,
'Don't send any material to me. You're not going to sing
on any songs. And shut the fuck up.' Basically that was it.
And that started the split between the brothers. Stu and I
stuck up for Tom and so we were in the doghouse as well.
And the business continued to fall apart. But John would
not give it up," said Clifford.

"Fantastic deals came across the board and he
turned them down. It was almost like he wanted to. Any
good offer that came was rejected. Anything bad, he did.
We had all of that going on at the time," said Clifford.

That dynamic among the band members,
exacerbated by the huge success it had experienced within
a short period of time in the late 1960s, set the stage for
the production of the group's fifth studio album.

And the title of the album was inspired by John
Fogerty's trepidation at dealing with the media.

17

The Vinyl Dialogues

"John wasn't comfortable with the press and my personality was — and always has been — I'm kind of the class clown, I like to have fun that way, tell stories. Keep things up and happy," said Clifford.

"So John called me upstairs and I thought, 'What the hell is going to happen now?' And he said, 'Look, I've decided to name the next release *Cosmo's Factory* and that's going to put the press over in your corner, and I wanted you to know why. You figure it out and keep them off my back. That's what I want to do.'

"And I said, 'Man, I can't wait!'" said Clifford. "I told different stories in different cities. It wasn't like it is now, everything, no matter where you are, gets out. You could tell one story in Chicago and a different story in another city. It was fun. I just had a lot of fun with it."

Cosmo's Factory became CCR's biggest album, selling more than four million copies. It was the No. 1 album for more than 12 weeks and had six singles, releasing them as three double-sided hits on 45 rpm records. In that era, double-sided hits on 45 rpm records were only common for artists like Elvis Presley, The Beatles, The Rolling Stones, and now, Creedence Clearwater Revival.

The album was released in July 1970 and included three double-sided hits: "Travelin' Band"/"Who'll Stop the Rain"; "Run Through the Jungle"/"Up Around the Bend"; and "Lookin' Out My Back Door"/"Long As I Can See the Light."

"The thing also was that we put out so much material in such a short period of time. Three albums in 1969 alone. And to make it even worse, we were cutting our singles in half. We could have stretched things out a little bit more. The reason why we were on such a pace was that John's theory was: If we were ever off the charts,

18

we'd be forgotten. Through that whole period of our career, we were never off the charts. We would release singles from the albums before the albums would be released. It was kind of backwards, really," said Clifford.

The quality of the music and the pace with which it was being released eventually proved to be too much.

"That made it really tough, because we were learning songs for albums and recording these albums didn't take long; it took us two weeks to do an album from start to finish. We'd rehearse and shape and work sides up for a couple of months, so the whole process was two-and-a-half months at the shortest. It was a wacky pace. And then we wanted to support those albums with touring and that put us on a wild pace for sure," said Clifford.

He suggested that the band hire a mentor.

"When you're in your early to mid-20s, you don't know much. And it was a wicked pace to keep up — there was a lot of pressure. The business side was going to hell in a hand basket; the brothers were at each other's throats. You think you know a lot and you really don't. In our case, we were in the big time and we didn't have guidance or any real professional management, somebody to smooth the problems out, use common sense, be someone that could mentor all of us. Smooth out the bumps, kick the record company's ass, all the things that needed to be done that were failing," he said.

"We had the biggest crumbling because of lack of management. But yet still we were producing at a ridiculous pace. That's what we did, hanging on by our fingernails trying to go on until it just blew up."

Of all the songs on *Cosmo's Factory*, Clifford said his favorite was CCR's version of "I Heard it Through the Grapevine." The song had originally come out of Berry Gordy's Motown and had been cut and released in 1967 by Gladys Knight and the Pips, reaching No. 2 on the Billboard chart. A year later, in 1968, Marvin Gaye's version of the song hit No. 1 on the Billboard pop singles chart and stayed there for seven weeks.

CCR's interpretation of the song was a little different. The version that ended up on *Cosmo's Factory* was 11:05 long, lengthened considerably from the original, just more than three minutes.

"We produced singles and we knew it, but we could also jam a little bit and that's what we did with 'Grapevine.' We did 11 covers of other people's music and that was my favorite one, because I got to do a little something that I normally didn't do and that's play a lot more fills, work a lot more with the lead guitar," said Clifford.

"That's sort of how I got my style. We'd play simple music, but any fill that I came up with had to be musical and any fill that John wanted me to do, it had to be musical, and if I didn't think it was the right fill, I'd argue. I'd fight for it. I won half the time and half the time I didn't," he said.

"But most of the time we would just jam on things and eventually things would fall into place and that's what we were doing. It was sort of a combination of things and our knack for coming up with musical ideas through those jams. We did it every day until we had an album together, and then we only worked on those songs. We didn't do 15 and pick 10; we did the number of songs that were on each album, and that is exactly what we worked on. No more and no less.

"So we knew going in before recording what the album was. Sometimes the songs weren't done lyrically and we didn't know what the lyrics were going to be until after the recording session and we heard what John had

20

come up with for the lyrics. It made it interesting because you don't really know," said Clifford.

"It was really a challenge; there is no question about that. Unfortunately, John had to be in charge of everything and in the end, it imploded the band. It was a very Shakespearean experience for a bunch of young guys, I'll tell you that."

Clifford said the band recorded "Grapevine" for FM radio, but it ended up making AM radio history.

"Here's the No. 1 singles band and they are stretching out one of the great classic songs of all time — just a brilliant song — and here we're going to take it 11 minutes and 5 seconds. This is what we're going to do, we're going to play this song and play it a lot. At that time we were at our peak, and it became the most-played, long track in AM radio history," said Clifford.

The album cover of *Cosmo's Factory* shows a photo of the latest incarnation of the factory at the time of the album's release, where the band rehearsed and worked on the songs for the album.

The photo includes the band members and their instruments, as well as some of their "man toys." John Fogerty is sitting at Clifford's drum set, while Clifford is shown sitting on his bicycle, wearing red sweatpants and a blue T-shirt, over which he has an orange tank top. An athlete, Clifford rode his bike every day to and from The Factory to work, seven-and-half miles each way.

"Once I knew this was going to be my namesake album, I wasn't going to wear jeans or running shorts; I was going to show off with some bright colors and some funny stuff. And I never wore it again," said Clifford.

A month after the picture was taken for the album cover, Clifford got hit by a car while riding that bike to work. He got scraped up quite a bit, but suffered no serious injuries, even though riders didn't wear bicycle helmets in those days.

"I eventually healed and I got another bike and crashed that one, too, and then decided I'd better start jogging because staying in shape was killing me," quipped Clifford.

Creedence Clearwater Revival broke up in 1972. Both John and Tom Fogerty went on to have solo careers, while Clifford and Cook still tour today as Creedence Clearwater Revisited. Tom died in 1990 from a tuberculosis infection. He had contracted HIV when he received a blood transfusion while being treated for back problems.

But *Cosmo's Factory* endures. CCR is still at the top of the rotation on classic rock radio stations.

"To me, that's our *Sgt. Pepper*. That's how I look at it," said Clifford. "I'm not comparing it to *Sgt. Pepper*; it's just how it fits in its place in our career. That ['Grapevine'] was our biggest hit and [*Cosmo's Factory*] my favorite album. It has quite a mixture — three cover songs and six singles. There's some great music there. And a couple of surprises. 'Ramble Tamble,' the opening song, is another interesting tune. Real exciting and then it has the gradual tempo change. And then it goes back up. It's an interesting tune to start out with, and then you go from there.

"We were pretty dedicated to the craft. It's the pinnacle of what we did. As an album standing up on its own, it's our best and most successful," he said.

American woman, stay away from Mrs. Nixon

American Woman
The Guess Who

*F*irst Lady Pat Nixon was throwing a party and she wanted some of the popular musicians of the times to provide the entertainment. It was the early 1970s and her husband, President Richard Nixon, hadn't yet been tainted by the Watergate scandal.

The party, held on the White House lawn, was a big deal. So big a deal, in fact, that the guests of honor were Britain's Princess Ann and Prince Charles, the British ambassador at the time, as well as the children of the biggest contributors to Richard Nixon's second successful presidential campaign.

The musical guests were Gary Puckett — who was performing with the U.S. Marines Band — and The Guess Who, a Canadian group that had scored three chart hits in 1970: "No Time," which reached No. 5, and "No Sugar Tonight" and "American Woman," both No. 1 singles, off the album *American Woman*, which reached No. 9 on the Billboard Pop Albums chart.

The Guess Who — which included Burton Cummings on lead vocals and guitar, Randy Bachman on guitar and vocals, Jim Kale on bass and vocals, and Garry Peterson on drums, percussion, and vocals — was hot. But the Nixon White House didn't want the band to play the song "American Woman" at the party because of its controversial lyrics that included references to the continued social unrest at the time, and the United States' involvement in the Vietnam War.

And the band agreed not to play it.

"I think someone in the White House — and you can be assured that it wasn't Mrs. Nixon — pointed out, and they were right, that 'American Woman' was a bit controversial because it wasn't about American women, it was about commentary," said Peterson, the original and current drummer of the Guess Who.

"But I guess Mrs. Nixon found out, and she said, 'Well, this is not appropriate, we can't have this.' So they came to our people and said, 'We would rather you not play this song.' And our attitude was, 'Fine. We're here to entertain people and make them feel good. We're not here to cause problems. So if you're hiring us and paying us and you don't want us to play our biggest hit, that's up to you,'" said Peterson.

"We didn't have any problems with that because we're a Canadian band. We weren't getting on a soapbox and saying, 'You shouldn't be in this war!'"

Peterson said it ended up being a great gig, despite the band not playing its biggest hit. Band members never left the White House lawn; they never entered the White House to look around or meet the President and Mrs. Nixon.

"I think Tricia Nixon [the President's daughter] was a fan, but I never got to talk to her," said Peterson. "We were no different than the security staff. We were hired and did our thing."

Peterson said that there were a lot of young adult children of U.S. senators on the guest list — kids who would have been fans of the popular music and culture of the times. And he did hear one story through the band's manager that caused him some concern at the time.

"They had round tables where you sat for dinner. I think one senator's daughter pulled out a bag of grass and put it on the table. Our manager went crazy and said, 'Are you nuts?' She could get by with it because she was a senator's daughter, but we were all Canadians with visas here in the States and all we needed was some kind of scandal like that," said Peterson.

The White House gig proved to be just one of the interesting aspects surrounding *American Woman*, The Guess Who's seventh album, and "American Woman," the single.

According to Peterson, the story of *American Woman* the album is not just about the single of the same name and how it got recorded in a studio in Chicago, but why it happened the way it did.

It was purely because until that point, the band wasn't getting the quality of recordings that it wanted, Peterson said. The two previous albums, *Wheatfield Soul* in 1968 and *Canned Wheat* in 1969, were produced by Jack Richardson and recorded in New York studios for record company RCA.

"But then RCA made a fateful mistake," said Peterson. "They wanted us to use their studio on the east side of New York, which was the studio where Woody Herman and Benny Goodman and all these guys — the big bands that were on RCA at the time — recorded. And the studio was ancient, with ancient equipment and ancient guys running it."

Canned Wheat was recorded at that studio and featured the singles "No Time," "Laughing," and "Undun."

"They're hits today, but they weren't [hits] on that album," Peterson said, "because the band was so unhappy with the sound on that album.

"And we thought, 'We're wasting good songs on this terrible-sounding album,'" said Peterson. Richardson made the decision to go back to A&R Recording, Inc. on West 48th Street and rerecord "Laughing" and "Undun."

"Those songs sound nothing like the rest of the [*Canned Wheat*] album," said Peterson. "And that's because they were done in a different studio than the one [the record company officials] forced us to use." That left the single "No Time" floundering on the *Canned Wheat* album. And the studio quality issues that The Guess Who were experiencing needed a solution, at least to the band's satisfaction.

"We needed a small, intimate studio," said Peterson. "Finally, Jack [Richardson] got RCA to allow us to look for a studio in its system and he found the one in Chicago — and that is the beginning of the *American Woman* album."

Peterson attributes the success of the *American Woman* album to the band bonding with a studio, in this instance with the RCA/Mid-America Recording Studio in Chicago.

"We did a lot of albums in that studio," said Peterson. "You have to be comfortable in the studio because you spend a lot of hours there. There are times when you run into the wall when recording and nothing sounds right and nothing works. We had a ping-pong table set up there. We had hockey sticks and we'd play ball hockey in the studio, just to kind of relieve the tension. Some days we got nothing done, but most of the time we really did well," he said.

The *American Woman* album was built around the single of the same name, and was essentially written by the band while onstage in what amounted to a jam session.

The band had gone back to Canada to do two shows just outside of Toronto. By that time, hits "These Eyes" and "Laughing" were placed on a double-sided 45 rpm record, which, according to Peterson, wasn't being done by many artists then.

"So we were a fairly big thing in Canada by that time. We were the local guys who had made good in the States. It was very tough to do that coming from a place like Winnipeg, the middle of nowhere, that wasn't particularly a media center," said Peterson.

"So we came back and played the shows. We had just done some extensive touring and we'd seen racial unrest in the United States," said Peterson. "We'd go into airports and there would be these young kids, soldiers going off to Vietnam. They were scared out of their minds. They didn't know what they were doing or where they were going, and they didn't know why. It wasn't like the other two wars [World Wars I and II] where you kind of knew what you were fighting for.

"We saw that, and we also saw them in airports coming back [from Vietnam], totally screwed up, with a glaze in their eyes. We saw the beginning of it and the end of it for a lot of young men.

"All of this, coming from Canada, which really didn't have those problems yet. It was foreign to us; we didn't know what to make of it. It was disturbing and frustrating on all those levels," said Peterson.

That highly charged political atmosphere in the U.S., and their unfamiliarity with it, were what the band members were dealing with on that night in the Toronto area where they were scheduled to play two shows. There were many bigwigs from RCA there, as was Richardson, the band's producer.

"It was quite a scene backstage. It was sort of a homecoming in a way for us," said Peterson. "And we took a break. When it was time to go back onstage, we couldn't find Burton [Cummings]. He was out talking to some fans and friends. So we decided to go back onstage and make some noise so Burton would hear that and come running."

At the time, Peterson was listening to the music of a band called The Electric Flag, and to Buddy Miles, who played double bass drums. There were a lot of great rhythmic sounds on the 1968 Electric Flag album *A Long Time Comin'* that appealed to Peterson.

"I started to play on the bass drum and then Randy [Bachman] started to play the guitar and so we were groovin' onstage," said Peterson. "Of course, Burton came running out and he just started to sing some words. I'm sure all this experience we had in the States resulted in him singing, 'American woman, stay away from me.' Because it wasn't about American women, it was about the country."

The crowd went nuts, and the band played the song at every gig from then on because it was becoming more and more successful.

"It was kind of like The Guess Who going harder rock. Not that we weren't. But we had ballads, 'These Eyes' and 'Laughing.' This gave us an opportunity to not be a ballad band," said Peterson.

"American Woman" refined itself and morphed. And then when the band was finally satisfied with the lyrics and the music, it went into the Chicago studio to record the single and the album.

"We didn't want to be a ballad band. Burton's favorite guy was Jim Morrison, so he wanted to be like Jim Morrison," said Peterson. "RCA said, 'Give us another ballad to solidify yourselves [which ended up being the re-recording of "No Time" off the *Canned Wheat* album that became the second cut on the *American Woman* album] and then you can do what you want to do.' In a sense, they were right and in a sense, we were right, too. It worked out well."

The album cover for *American Woman* features the faces of the four band members superimposed over a colorized photo of a woman's face.

"RCA was a corporate company and it did its own thing," said Peterson. "Now we had the right of refusal, and a lot of times the corporate guys came up with covers that we didn't want. But we liked this one." The back of the album features a photo of the band members in an ice cream shop in New York City, taken by a staff photographer for RCA.

"Of course the studio wanted you to use its staff. Why wouldn't we have gotten one of the most famous rock photographers of the time? Because we would have had to pay for that ourselves," said Peterson.

But Peterson thinks the inside cover of the album is far more interesting. It features the lyrics to the songs on the record over the top of "ghosted" photos provided by each of the band members.

"That's all our baby pictures. Go to the top left corner, that's me and my mom. She knitted that sweater for me," said Peterson. "Go to the lefthand side, bottom right. Look very closely. There's a little guy with a cowboy hat and a little car. That's a Jeep my father made

29

for me. I'm about three years old there. Those are all our baby pictures and nobody knows that.

"People have had that album for more than 40 years and they still don't know that. They're busy focusing on the lyrics."

Even after all the years that have passed, Peterson still believes that the demise of the original band was about money, ego, and greed.

"The biggest song we ever had ['American Woman'] you could say was a collaboration onstage," said Peterson. "What's the only No. 1 song the band ever had? 'American Woman,' although arguably the flip side, which was 'No Sugar Tonight,' charted No. 1 at the same time. So it was a double-sided No. 1 record. The only other [musicians who] ever did that were Elvis, The Beatles, and The Rolling Stones. I'm not saying we're in that company, but just for that one thing we were, and that's something that nobody can ever take away from us.

"But we really never did that again. We all put ['American Woman'] together on stage. Arguably Burton came up with the lyrics because he sang them on stage every night and he tried to do something different. But nobody ever came to us and said, 'Why don't we sit down and write a song together?' None of the songwriters [Cummings and Bachman] ever wanted to do that and I know in my heart it was because once you did that, you had to share the credit and there was less money for them.

"I didn't know it at the time, I was just happy to be a team member," said Peterson. "You look at some of the bigger bands that are successful and they have always taken care of all their members. The ones that aren't successful didn't take care of all their members.

"The two writers, Randy and Burton, could have changed that. We could have done a group song on every album and it would have given a source of revenue to the other guys. I would have done that. And why? Because when everybody is happy, everybody is happy," said Peterson. "And that's the reason the band broke up, I believe. I don't say this with malice. I wish nothing but the best for everybody in the band."

As for the creative aspect of recording in the late 1960s and early 1970s, Peterson said it was a simpler time, when bands were allowed to develop and create.

"We were very fortunate in that we were recording in a era where we were allowed to do just about anything," he said. "The corporate mark of what is the formula for selling was not refined the way it is now.

"I feel very fortunate in my life to have been able to do what I have done. And I'm still doing it."

It only takes one toke to make the enemies list

Tarkio
Brewer & Shipley

t started with a block of hashish in the Vanguard, a little club in Kansas City. It ended with a hit song that landed the songwriters on President Richard Nixon's infamous "Enemies List" for being subversives. Ironically, at the same time, that same tune was being hailed as a "modern day spiritual" by squeaky-clean television bandleader Lawrence Welk.

The folk-rock duo of Michael Brewer and Tom Shipley took positions as staff songwriters for A&M Records in Los Angeles in the late 1960s. But when they had pretty much had it with the L.A. music scene, they headed back to their roots in Missouri to make a living touring the heartland, which is how they ended up at the Vanguard in Kansas City, getting high before a performance.

"Somebody had given me a block of hash. And he said do two hits, and I did three," said Tom Shipley. "And I go out of the dressing room — I'm also a banjo player, but I didn't have one, so I was playing my guitar — and Michael came in and I said, 'Jesus, Michael, I'm one toke over the line.' And to be perfectly honest, I don't remember if Michael was with me when I took that hit or not. I remember it as "not;" I think Michael remembers it as "yes." And he started to sing to what I was playing, and

33

I chimed in and boom, we had the line."

Michael Brewer remembers it pretty much the same way.

"I just cracked up. I thought it was hysterical," said Brewer. "And right on the spot, we just started singing, 'One toke over the line, sweet Jesus,' and that was about it; then we went onstage.

"The next day we got together to do some pickin' and I thought, 'What was that last night that we were messing with?' And in about an hour we turned it into a song. We literally wrote that song to make our friends and ourselves laugh, period. We didn't even take it seriously; it was just something to make our friends laugh."

As it turned out, Brewer and Shipley would be laughing all the way to the bank on the back of "One Toke Over the Line."

At the time, the duo was working on its third album, *Tarkio*, which would be released in 1970. They were booked to play Carnegie Hall in New York for the first time, opening for the singer-songwriter Melanie Anne Safka, known professionally simply as Melanie. In 1972, Melanie had a No. 1 song, "Brand New Key," often called "The Roller Skate Song."

"It was the first time we played Carnegie Hall and it went over really well. We got two or three encores and basically ran out of songs," said Brewer. "So we decided, 'Let's do that new song.' We had nothing to lose. So we did 'One Toke' and it went over like gangbusters. And the president of the record company we were with [Kama Sutra Records] came backstage and said, 'Aw, man, it's a great song. You gotta record that and add it to the album.' Which kind of took us by surprise because we didn't even take it seriously."

In fact, Brewer and Shipley didn't have any plans at all for "One Toke Over the Line," let alone inclusion on the unfinished *Tarkio* album. It was just another song to them, albeit one with a catchy tune. Mostly, what they did was scratch their heads, wondering how that song was getting any traction at all.

But it may have been a sign of the times. The hippie folk scene was in full swing by the end of the 1960s.

"Essentially there was a whole generation in motion at that time," said Shipley. "Everybody was out, everybody was traveling, everybody was in their Volkswagen Beetles or vans. I had one of those old Volvos that had like a bathtub back to it. If it wasn't for national forest parks and national forest campgrounds and Indian reservations, I would have been homeless.

"But you ran into a lot of other people who were exactly like you. They were headed back from a summer of love or trying to leave someplace. We were writing about what was happening to us. And I think the success was that we were writing about the same thing that was happening to everybody else," said Shipley.

Brewer & Shipley's second album, *Weeds*, released in 1969, was what they both consider to be essentially a double-album, along with *Tarkio,* which was released the following year.

"It was more than just a group of songs. If you were to take the two albums, *Weeds* and *Tarkio*, and play them back to back, it wouldn't necessarily be linear, but you would get a pretty good idea of not only what was happening in our lives but in the lives of those in our generation," he said.

"We were just at the right place at the right time in a lot of ways," said Brewer. "We, along with a number of other artists, of course, helped create folk rock. And with our *Weeds* and *Tarkio* albums, it was a real hybrid. In *Tarkio*, we were also incorporating a little bit of country. You know, country was changing; it's folk, it's rock, it's country. In fact, people had a hard time categorizing us at the time because it was something new and there wasn't a category.

"It was a magical period for music. The late '60s and the early '70s kind of all goes together. Buffalo Springfield formed in the house next door to me in Hollywood. There was just so much music going on. It was all just a bunch of struggling musicians who wanted to get a record deal, who wanted to make music and were starting to write songs of their own," he said.

The song "One Toke Over the Line" brought attention to the album *Tarkio*, which in turn exposed people to Brewer & Shipley's previous works — the duo's debut *Down in L.A.*, released in 1968, and their second album, *Weeds*.

But "One Toke Over the Line" also got the government's attention because of the drug reference. In fact, then-Vice President Spiro Agnew was naming names, and Brewer & Shipley's were on the list.

"Agnew came out and railed on us for being subversives to American youth and all that stuff," said Shipley. "And what got me then was that radio stations started to pull back from it. Wait a second; all of a sudden we have a hit. Nope, what's happening to it? Stations were starting to drop the song."

"You gotta remember this was when the government was making the FCC threaten radio stations with pulling their licenses if they didn't edit so-called drug lyrics in rock and roll," said Brewer. "It was equivalent [to] burning books. It was just ridiculous. That included songs like 'Puff the Magic Dragon' and 'Eight Miles High.' It was just crazy."

At that moment, Chicago was a hotbed of hullabaloo regarding the government's threats to the FCC. As luck would have it, Brewer and Shipley were playing a gig at a place called the Quiet Night in Chicago, while the National Association of Broadcasters' convention was being held in Chicago as well. Some of the broadcasters from the convention sat in the audience for the Brewer & Shipley show that evening.

"The song ['One Toke'] was kind of a cause celebre at the time, not officially banned, but they [the FCC] were threatening radio stations with pulling their licensing," said Shipley.

So when it came time to sing "One Toke Over the Line" that evening, Brewer & Shipley dedicated the song to Chicago native Newton Minow, who was sitting in the audience. Minow was the FCC's chairman when the regulatory agency was threatening radio stations about airing drug-related lyrics.

"And he kind of half-stood up and said, 'I always liked you guys; you took me wrong.' I might not know much, but I knew how to handle a guy in the audience who had too much to drink," said Shipley.

After the show, Brewer and Shipley headed back toward their dressing room where a group of broadcasters — and Minow — were hanging around.

"And this guy from the FCC, he comes up and puts his arm around me and again he says, 'I always liked you guys. I can't believe that they all took my words wrong.' As soon as he said that, I spun around and just nose-to-nose said, 'You're the head of the FCC. You have access to ABC, NBC, CBS, and all the other media. If they took your words wrong, isn't your duty to set the record straight?" said Shipley.

The next day the general manager of ABC radio called Brewer and Shipley into his office and said, "Are you guys trying to promote drugs?"

"And I said, 'Listen to the lyrics. It's a song about excess.' We had used a street term, 'toked,' and that's what had them freaked. They didn't bother to actually listen to the lyrics," said Shipley.

"So he said, 'OK, we're staying on it.' Then the other radio stations started coming back on the record. But by that point it was — you know how hit records go, they can go up and down — when you're hot, you're hot, and when you're not, you're not. And all this happened just kind of at the song's peak and just enough stations had gone off of it. It hurt overall sales; I'll put it that way. But at the same time, I had coined a phrase that is part of Americana now. I feel kind of good about that. I wouldn't trade that for money at this point," said Shipley.

But Brewer and Shipley weren't done with the government just yet. In fact, Brewer and Shipley disliked Nixon so much that they named him in a song — also included on the album *Tarkio* — called "Oh Mommy (I Ain't No Commie)." The distinctive steel guitar on that tune was played by Jerry Garcia of the Grateful Dead.

Brewer said that he and Shipley fully expected some repercussions at the time from the government, but nothing ever happened. That didn't mean there weren't some chilling moments associated with the fallout, however.

One of those moments occurred in 1971 when Brewer and Shipley were scheduled to appear on *The David Frost Show*, along with CBS newsman, Mike

Wallace. CBS had aired a documentary called *The Selling of the Pentagon* by filmmaker Peter Frank Davis. And the Nixon administration was none too happy with CBS, Wallace, and Davis, just as it had been none too happy about Brewer & Shipley's "One Toke Over the Line."

"And [Wallace] told me backstage that the Nixon administration was essentially trying, through intimidation, to get control of the media. They were very paranoid and they didn't like what the media was saying about them, so they were bullies and they were trying to intimidate people in all sorts of media," said Shipley.

"I took Mike Wallace at his word. At that point I got a little scared. The ACLU had wanted Michael and I to take it to court and all this stuff, and we kept saying, 'It's a joke. We were trying to make ourselves and our close friends laugh. Period.' It was a joke and we didn't want to make it anything more serious than that," he said.

"But when Mike Wallace was talking about what was happening with the media, he was being very serious. They [the government] were just threatening to pull our record off the air. They were threatening to do way more than that to him. He was in politics, more or less, so he was much more serious about it than I was. But he made my blood run cold," said Shipley.

After all that attention from the government, "One Toke Over the Line" also got a different kind of attention, this time from Lawrence Welk, who didn't appear to have the same take on the song as did the U.S. government. Singers Gail Farrell and Dick Dale performed the song on *The Lawrence Welk Show* in 1971. After the performance, Welk said, "There you heard a modern spiritual by Gail and Dale."

"We were in London at the time, so we didn't see it or even believe it," said Brewer. "But it was verified because my mom saw it. And my brother just happened to be walking through the room and when it came on, everybody just stopped and stared at the TV. And my brother said Mom was saying, 'No, no, no, Lawrence.'"

"I was amazed, but at the same time I was also on the road and smoking a lot of pot, so I could believe just about anything," said Shipley.

It took Brewer & Shipley more than 35 years to find a copy of "One Toke Over the Line" being performed on *The Lawrence Welk Show*. They finally tracked down a woman in Branson, Missouri — where Welk had a theater — who was in charge of archiving all the Welk shows.

"We thought once they'd realized what they had done they had deleted it from their archives," said Brewer. "But she got a copy of it and Tom immediately put it on YouTube for the whole world to see."

"I made the mistake of posting it on my YouTube site and I'm trying desperately to find a way to not be notified every time somebody makes a comment now," said Shipley. "It just keeps filling up my email [inbox]. But at the same time, I'm reticent to pull it down because so many folks like it."

The essential evolution of Brewer & Shipley's second album *Weeds*, which continued through the third album, *Tarkio*, and the success fueled by "One Toke Over the Line," was among the duo's best work, according to Brewer.

"Our albums aren't just a bunch of songs. We never released an album that wasn't an album as such. A lot of thought goes into which songs are used and the flow, the sequence of the songs," said Brewer. "There's more to listening to a Brewer & Shipley album than just songs. At least that's always been our intention."

Shipley agreed that their music had more to offer than the scope of just one single that got a lot of attention.

"I think people looked at our other songs seriously," he said. "But I'm glad my life turned out exactly like it has turned out. God knows what would have happened if one of those other songs would have been a hit. In the grand scheme of things, Michael and I became known for 'One Toke Over the Line' instead of what I thought was the kind of stuff that we did best.

"You got to understand that, to me, it's *Weeds* and *Tarkio*. I couldn't be prouder of them. I think it's interesting to see where our heads were at. We were artists up through *Tarkio* and once *Tarkio* hit, we went from being artists to [being] commodities. So what was the name of the next album? *Shake Off the Demon*. Because we had become commodities and the only way we could stay sane as commodities was to do all that stuff you read about in *Rolling Stone*. Which, fortunately, didn't kill us," said Shipley.

Little more than the last record

Search and Nearness
The Rascals

*T*he Rascals were done and they knew it. Eddie Brigati had left the group in late 1970, but before doing so, he recorded some vocals for what was to be the band's final album, *Search and Nearness*, which wouldn't be released until March 1971.

The remaining members — Dino Danelli, Gene Cornish, and Felix Cavaliere – wanted to give Brigati a proper sendoff, despite the fact that the band had imploded and each would be going his separate way after the album's release. They decided to use the imagery inside the cover of the album to say goodbye to Brigati.

The band had an office in a building on 32nd Street in New York City. Danelli, Cornish, and Cavaliere hired a photographer, and on the roof of the office building, shot some photos that could be considered for use as cover art for their album.

As an artist as well as a musician, Danelli had long had an interest in the aesthetics of an album cover, and in fact, had a hand in conceptualizing and creating much of the band's album cover art over the years.

"We were on the roof just hanging, and in the city, you sometimes see sneakers hanging on wires," said Danelli, the band's drummer. "And there they were. So we

43

took these sneakers off the wire and we put them on the roof and we sat around them. Then Gene put his arm up, like it would be around Eddie's shoulder if he were there, and we took that shot."

On a building in the background of the photo, an image of Brigati was superimposed into one of the windows. Even though he had left, Brigati was still a part of the group for this album as far as the other band members were concerned.

"It was fun," said Danelli. "And it was saying goodbye with love to Eddie at that point."

The shot was used on the inner cover of *Search and Nearness*. But it wasn't the only art on the album that was influenced by Danelli. The front cover of the album also featured a Danelli-inspired piece of art.

"I was very interested in surrealist art at that particular time and that was a cover done by Wolfgang Hutter," said Danelli. "It's a young girl with wings and it's very artistically psychedelic. It had a different vibe, a much more sophisticated kind of surrealism."

Danelli considered using three or four different pieces of art by Hutter for the cover, but eventually settled on the image of the young girl with wings.

"It was just where I was in my head at that point in my experiences," said Danelli. "It did symbolize a little bit of the change that was going on in life at the time, and it was stunning. I loved that cover."

"We were pretty much a broken-up band," said Danelli when *Search and Nearness* was released. It was the seventh and last album The Rascals recorded for Atlantic Records.

"We knew that we were leaving Atlantic. We were having problems not only within the band, but with the record label," he said.

Danelli said The Rascals just weren't generating what Atlantic had come to expect from a band that had produced three No. 1 hits — "Good Lovin'" in 1966, "Groovin'" in 1967, and "People Got to Be Free" in 1968 — and a bunch of other Top 40 hits along the way.

"We were heavily influenced by the counterculture that existed at that point and they [Atlantic officials] didn't like that at all," said Danelli. "They wanted us to get back into The Rascals from early on — the love and party stuff — that kind of vibe. But we just weren't there anymore. We had moved on and everybody [in the band] was just experiencing life. Everybody was a different person."

Since it was going to be the last album The Rascals recorded for Atlantic, the company didn't put a lot of money behind its promotion and distribution. It barely charted on the Billboard Top 200, coming in at No. 198.

Brigati is not listed as a member of the group, although he is credited as the lead vocalist on three songs: "You Don't Know" penned by Cornish; a cover of "The Letter" by The Box Tops; and "Fortunes," written by Danelli.

In the end, though, Danelli said that *Search and Nearness* was little more than "the last record."

And more than 40 years later, nothing appears to have changed about the perception of the music on *Search and Nearness*.

After decades of trying, Steven Van Zandt — of Bruce Springsteen and the E Street Band fame — finally reunited the original members of The Rascals. The band had a strong influence on a young Van Zandt in the 1960s, and through the years, he believed that they had never been properly recognized as one of the great bands of that decade.

So Van Zandt and his wife, Maureen, wrote, co-directed and co-produced the show *Once Upon A Dream* — taken from the band's fourth studio album of the same name in 1968 — and called it a "BioConcert" starring Danelli, Cornish, Cavaliere, and Brigati in an innovative, Broadway-like show. It featured a multimedia presentation that told the story of The Rascals, using young actors portraying the principals, visual storytelling, and a big-time light and design production by Marc Brickman, all woven into a concert featuring approximately 30 songs performed by the original members.

"I get a chance to thank The Rascals for what they've meant to me, and at the same time, make sure their place in history is assured," said Van Zandt. "It didn't feel to me like that was the case, so I needed to do this show and tell everybody their story. I wanted to show the wide breadth of talent that exists in these songs. These guys are absolutely remarkable and I want them from now on to be mentioned in the same sentence as The Beatles, The Rolling Stones, and The Byrds," said Van Zandt.

In addition to the hits, Van Zandt intentionally included about a dozen songs in the show that only die-hard Rascals fans would recognize.

"People were surprised that I did that, but when they see the show they understand," said Van Zandt. "But the songs are so good that they are immediately accessible, even if you're hearing them for the first time.

"They're very deep, either exploring various kinds of rhythms or chord changes, or maybe they're a bit more jazzy or a bit more improv, whatever it might be," he said.

And still, not one song from the *Search and Nearness* album, even four decades later, made the cut. Just maybe, though, the band made a greater contribution than just its music. Van Zandt certainly thinks so.

"We're being invaded with negativity 24 hours a day. All we hear is bad news," said Van Zandt. "And you know, to hear The Rascals records, which embodied the spirit of the '60s, is to once again experience optimism and love and brotherhood, words that we just don't use anymore or see any evidence of anymore.

"I was just trying to capture their moment and contribution to history," he said. "But I realized that in that contribution, there is something bigger than their music and bigger than the group itself. And that is the ideals that decade communicated.

Because they broke up in 1970, [the band] was never anything else, which is wonderful. It was never diluted, it was never compromised. It didn't have to be, because they left when the '60s left. So when you see them now, you're seeing the '60s in all of its glory, in all of its optimism, in all of its love and color. It's right there," said Van Zandt.

And even with the benefit of more than 40 years of hindsight, maybe *Search and Nearness* is destined to remain simply "the last record" in a body of work that is something much more.

The Rascals — Eddie Brigati, Felix Cavaliere, Gene Cornish
and Dino Danelli — reunited in 2013 for a 13-city East Coast
tour titled *Once Upon A Dream* — taken from a 1968 Rascals
album of the same name — described as a "BioConcert." The
show was a multimedia Broadway-like presentation that
combined a concert by the original Rascals with video
reminiscences and a light show. Top photo: drummer Dino
Danelli and guitarist Gene Cornish rock out. Middle:
Keyboardist Felix Cavaliere and Cornish perform for a packed
house at the Philadelphia Academy of Music in June 2013.
Bottom photo: Danelli keeps the beat against the red
background. (Photos by Mike Morsch)

Neither the nod nor the wink have anything to do with the music

A Nod Is as Good as a Wink
. . . to a Blind Horse
Faces

Paul McCartney was a bit of a prude. At least that's how Ian McLagan saw him in late 1971. McLagan, keyboardist for the band Faces, and his bandmates — Ronnie Lane, Kenney Jones, Ronnie Wood, and Rod Stewart — had just released their third album, *A Nod Is as Good as a Wink . . . to a Blind Horse*, which included a poster featuring a collage of personal pictures submitted by each member of the band, as well as road crew members.

The poster was the brainchild of Mike McInnerney, an artist and photographer whose successes include the 1969 pop-art, triptych-style fold-out cover for The Who's fourth album, *Tommy.*

McInnerney, who had photographed the Faces' members for the band's debut album, *First Step,* in 1970, lived just up the street in London from Faces' bassist Lane. When the band was cutting *A Nod Is as Good as a Wink . . . to a Blind Horse*, McInnerney suggested that a poster be made and distributed with the album.

"Mike thought it would be good if we handed him all of our photographs," said McLagan. "Of course, he asked the road crew (for photographs) as well, and the road crew had nothing but pornographic pictures (of

49

groupies). Ours were family shots and others, like me, on the toilet. That's nice."

McInnerney then put all the photos together — and added a few other images he thought gave the piece some pizzazz — to create the collage featured on the poster.

"Paul McCartney came around — because the album was just finished — to Ronnie's flat and we played him the album," said McLagan. "But when he saw the poster, he was disgusted. There were photographs of bottles of brandy just taken from ads. I don't know why Mike did that. There are probably about 100 pictures on this thing, most of them just Polaroids and shit. Mike also took photographs of ads for pills — I don't know what pills, they might have been headache pills or birth control pills — and they were included as well.

"We didn't like that," said McLagan. "We didn't think it was very clever, but it was Mike's take on us. Paul was disgusted. He was a bit of a prude. It was so funny."

The poster was initially released with the album, but the record company, Warner Brothers, had second thoughts and eventually re-released the album without the poster. Because so few of the posters got out into the general public, they are considered collectors' items today.

"There was a little bit of a fuss about it," deadpans McLagan. "Which is exactly what we wanted."

Of the band's four albums, *A Nod Is as Good as a Wink . . . to a Blind Horse* was its most successful, reaching No. 6 on the Billboard chart. And it contained the group's most successful single, "Stay with Me," which made it to No. 17 on the U.S. charts and all the way to No. 6 on the United Kingdom charts.

The name of the album was Lane's idea, according
to McLagan.

"I'm really proud of that record," said McLagan.
"But the name was all Ronnie Lane. It means you can nod
or wink at a blind horse; it doesn't make any difference.
It's just a funny expression. It's a little bit London. And it
doesn't have a damn thing to do with the music."

The Faces had produced their first two albums —
First Step in 1970 and *Long Player* in early 1971 — but
for *A Nod Is as Good as a Wink . . . to a Blind Horse*, they
brought in Glyn Johns to co-produce. Johns also produced
the band's fourth and final album, *Ooh La La,* in 1973.

"Glyn came in to produce and it shows on our
albums," said McLagan. "Suddenly, our albums weren't a
bunch of songs thrown together."

McLagan said that what was great about Johns
was that in addition to being an incredible sound engineer,
he was also a great producer.

"He could look into the future a little bit," said
McLagan. "He encouraged all of us. Rod was kind of a
dominating force, but Glyn wasn't buying that, and it was
a good thing for Rod. Glyn got us all feeling good about
ourselves in the studio and it made us more productive.
And we had a damn good time, too."

McLagan said that the technical aspect of what
Johns brought to the table — as both an engineer and a
producer — is what helped improve the later Faces
albums.

"A lot of engineers, when you go into the studio,
they'll say, 'Well, play this song,'" said McLagan. "And
we'd play a little bit and go, 'OK, we've got a good
sound.'

"And then we'd go in to mix it and it would sound like shit. And we'd think, 'Why didn't the engineer come into the studio and hear the piano live with his ears?'

"That's what Glyn would do. He'd come in and say, 'Hmmm. All right, I like that sound. It's a beautiful piano.' And then he'd go into the control room and try to make sure that was the sound he got.

"That was Glyn; he was very diligent," recalls McLagan. "He'd come out and tweak my amp; he'd tweak the piano volume. Then he would go back into the control room and make sure that was the sound he wanted."

Coincidentally, Johns was elected into the Rock and Roll Hall of Fame in 2012, the same year that Faces was inducted.

Although "Stay with Me" is the single most remembered from *A Nod Is as Good as a Wink . . . to a Blind Horse*, McLagan likes the second cut on the album, a song he wrote with Lane titled "You're So Rude." It was written at a house that McLagan owned in Kingston, near London.

"What was going to be my studio in that house had a rising damp in the walls, so I had all the plaster and floorboards pulled out and replaced," said McLagan. "I was going to put a tile floor in there. So while that was going on, I had this huge harmonium pump organ that would have gone in the studio, but I had to have it in the hallway.

"So when you came in the front door, you kind of had to ease your way past it," he said. "So I had it out there and I had this melody and Ronnie came over. I played him 'You're So Rude' but there were no lyrics.

"And he said, 'Oh, that's fantastic.' And he sat down and wrote the lyrics out in one go. I still have that sheet of paper. He made only one correction, but it was just a grammatical thing."

McLagan said the lyrics are a true story about Lane's first girlfriend.

"It actually happened," recalls McLagan. "'I'll wet my socks, pretend we just got caught in the rain.' Yeah, right. But it worked.

"I met her soon after I joined Small Faces [the band that preceded Faces]. She wasn't Ronnie's girlfriend anymore, but she was friendly. She was a pretty girl.

"Ronnie was a brilliant writer like that," said McLagan. "That's the whole secret of writing, I think . . . that you keep writing. John Mellencamp once said, 'You keep the doors and windows open so you're always aware.'"

Lane left the band in 1973, and died in 1997 from complications of multiple sclerosis.

In addition to the four albums it released, Faces toured regularly until 1975, when it officially disbanded. At the same time, Stewart was pursuing a solo career, which partially hastened Lane's departure from the band. And toward the end, Wood was touring with The Rolling Stones, whom he joined after Faces officially disbanded.

After the split, McLagan worked as a sideman for The Rolling Stones and with other artists such as Bob Dylan, Bruce Springsteen, Jackson Browne, Melissa Etheridge, Chuck Berry, and Joe Cocker.

Since 1977, he has released several solo albums, and his own group — The Bump Band — still plays regularly at the Lucky Lounge in Austin, Texas, McLagan's adopted hometown in the United States.

The one thing he never stopped doing was writing songs and touring to showcase his music.

"Live music is the future of rock and roll as far as I'm concerned," said McLagan. "It's about dealing with people coming out to hear a show which is never going to be repeated, even if you play the same songs in the same order.

"I went to see the Stones in L.A. while I was out there and they were fantastic," he said. "I then went to see Paul McCartney — just fantastic. I mean, Jesus Christ, the energy of Mick Jagger. And Paul . . . he's singing unbelievable, he's playing unbelievable."

McLagan's autobiography, *All the Rage: A Riotous Romp Through Rock and Roll History*, was originally released in 1998 and re-released in 2013. And he's got 30 to 40 songs — some of which he's had around for years — that still aren't finished.

"But I never give up on them," he said. "A writer without a pen is a reader.

"What I do remember [about the Faces years] — and what I love about writing — is when you sit down to write about certain situations, and as you're writing, you're in that room and you're in that space. It just opens up. I was always fascinated with that, so I didn't want to stop."

Today, McLagan admits he'd certainly like to play big venues and earn lots of money, but he's quite content to be up close and personal with his audiences.

"I play to people who give a damn," he said. "They come out to be told a few stories and hear some tunes. And I always play the Ronnie Lane songs and a bunch of my own songs. I talk a lot and I enjoy talking. There are stories to be told and funny things to enjoy."

And then there's the fun. There's always been the fun — starting with Small Faces, then Faces, and

54

everything that's happened since *A Nod Is as Good as a Wink . . . to a Blind Horse* was released in 1971.

"We had the best time. Someone was just saying the other day, 'You guys must have been having big fun!' And I said, 'Absolutely. It's true.'

"As soon as I stop having fun, I don't know what I'll do," said McLagan. "I'll just have to sort of walk quietly into the woods."

Crazy and creative arrangements using a garbage can

Harmony
Three Dog Night

The middle of 1971 was a crazy period for Three Dog Night. So when it came time to record their next album, *Harmony*, band members decided to show how crazy they could get: They used a garbage can to create some of the most remarkable music in the group's history.

Three Dog Night had been touring non-stop in the early 1970s. Its lead singers — Danny Hutton, Chuck Negron, and Cory Wells — alternated singing lead on their songs. They were backed by Jimmy Greenspoon on organ, Floyd Sneed on drums, Mike Allsup on guitar, and Joe Schermie on bass.

"Just when we started *Harmony*, out of nowhere, 'Joy to the World' took off like a rocket," said Hutton.

Written by Hoyt Axton, Three Dog Night's version of "Joy to the World" ended up a No. 1 hit and was on the band's fifth studio album, *Naturally*, released in November 1970.

"It was six weeks at No. 1. It was crazy. We thought it was some fluke the first week and then it just stayed there forever," said Hutton. "And before that song went back down the charts, then 'Liar' became a hit. All of a sudden it was a crazy period."

"Liar," written by Russ Ballard, reached No. 7 on the charts and gave Three Dog Night its second Top 10 hit off the *Naturally* album.

Also on the *Naturally* album was the song "Heavy Church," written by Alan O'Day, a sophisticated, multilayered song.

"We spent such a long time on it. It was so intricate. Bill Cooper [the album's engineer] had this crazy system of trying to keep the tracks all in your head. We had a lot of overdubs, but in a good way. So it was very layered," said Hutton.

The combination of the heavy touring schedule, the success of two Top Ten singles, and the complex experience of making the song "Heavy Church," set the stage as Three Dog Night began to make its seventh studio album, *Harmony*.

In mid-1971, between *Naturally* and *Harmony,* the band released the album *Golden Bisquits*, a compilation of hits from the band's first four studio albums.

But the groundwork laid with *Naturally* provided a fertile environment for the band to kick it up a notch in the creativity department for *Harmony*, which eventually led to a garbage can being used to make music.

"When we talked about doing the [*Harmony*] album, we talked about that. It was time to kind of expand and just really get into way more intricate tracks, not just be limited by being a four-piece band so we could do everything live. We said let's just get crazy and creative," said Hutton.

So that was the plan for *Harmony* when it came to production and arrangements — crazy and creative.

"Heavy Church" incorporated all the elements of that template.

"That's the one where we ended up trying to get this guitar sound with one of those voice-bags, like [Peter] Frampton uses, with a big, long tube," said Hutton. "We spent forever trying to get that sound. What we ended up doing was Michael [Allsup] had his guitar and then he had the voice-bag with the long tube that you usually stuck in your mouth to make your guitar talk.

"We ended up putting the tube into a big garbage can, which I spun, and that's the sound," said Hutton. "We did that all the time. We would go into bathrooms to find a sound. The philosophy was, if you had a wah-wah pedal, don't put it on a guitar and use it like it's supposed to be used; put it on the organ. Always do something different with the instruments. It was a lot of fun trying to get arrangements to be different using a variety of sounds.

"If you hear 'Heavy Church,' it's just amazing, the overdubs and different parts. We loved that song. We just thought, let's go for something bigger than just three singers and a four-piece band. We just thought we'd stretch out."

As much as the band members liked that song, it's not the big hit off the *Harmony* album. *Harmony*, released in late December 1971, featured two other songs that cracked the Top 10, "An Old Fashioned Love Song," written by Paul Williams, which charted at No. 4, and "Never Been to Spain," another Axton-penned tune, which charted at No. 5.

On the strength of those two songs — and "The Family of Man," written by Williams and Jack Conrad, which just missed being a third Top 10 hit, checking in at No. 12 — the album itself reached No. 8 on the charts.

The band members had a feeling that "An Old Fashioned Love Song" was going to be a hit.

"As you well know, there is my version, somebody else's version, and then the truth," said Hutton. "What I remember about that song is that we'd have these listening sessions with a bunch of demos. And that was one we heard and all went, 'Yeah, that's cool.'"

Hutton recalls that he had to leave town at one point during the recording sessions for *Harmony*, and when he returned, Negron had finished "An Old Fashioned Love Song."

"Originally what I remember was that Chuck and I were going to take turns singing leads on verses. But I came back and Chuck had done all the verses. He said, 'Oops, you weren't here, man. I think it works better with just me.' But we didn't have the outro for that song. So I arranged that part," said Hutton.

It wasn't a surprise to Hutton that "An Old Fashioned Love Song" hit big. Songwriter Williams had been on a roll in the early 1970s, having written hit singles for The Carpenters — "We've Only Just Begun" in 1970 and "Rainy Days and Mondays" in 1971.

"Paul Williams at the time was so hot with The Carpenters, so that didn't hurt when the deejays looked at the album and saw his name on the song, they went, 'Whoa, let's check this out,'" said Hutton. "We wanted to be a rock band. But once in a while you do something like that and it's like, 'Oh my God.'"

Negron's version of the story isn't much different.

"When I heard 'An Old Fashioned Love Song,' the publishers weren't really that hot on it because they had Paul Williams writing with different people and he was very successful," said Negron. "This was the first time he had written by himself.

"So I said, 'Play it for me, I want to hear it.' I heard it and I said, 'Hey, this is a good song.'"

When it comes to recollections about *Harmony's* other hit, "Never Been to Spain," the song has a similar vibe.

"There's a couple of stories. Some of the guys remember it as Hoyt coming in and playing us the demo, and even before it was finished, we went, 'Yeah!' I can't say that did happen or it didn't happen," said Hutton.

"But Cory has this whole story about him going up north and I guess Hoyt had a cabin somewhere, so they went fishing together. And then they came back to the cabin and Hoyt had the wine set up and the fireplace going and played the song for him there. It was much more romantic. I can't say that didn't happen."

According to Hutton, the challenge with Axton's material was that Axton had a big baritone voice and he basically strummed the guitar. He wasn't a lead guitar player guy.

"He played a lot of little arrangement licks in the middle of his playing. So you had to kind of really get through that. It was a low key. But we knew his lyrics were always wonderful, simple but clever. The hardest thing to do is a simple song that doesn't have a lot of really fancy chords and he could deliver that," said Hutton.

For "Never Been to Spain," the band decided to use a steel guitar.

"So we called Rusty Young from Poco. I think Timothy B. Schmidt [from the Eagles] was in the group [Poco] then. So Rusty came over in his pajamas and he was just great on it. He was so fast and wonderful. We released the album and forgot to mention him. He didn't get any credit. But then on the next album we gave him credit . . . for the song he had done on the previous album," said Hutton.

"The funniest thing is, you know the *Captured Live at the Forum* [released in 1969] album, if you open that up and look, there's credit to the four musicians, and we forgot to give ourselves credit, the three singers. Our names aren't even on there. We were always asleep at the wheel . . . or drunk or whatever."

When he hears the original recording of "Never Been to Spain" now, Hutton thinks it's way too slow.

"We do it better time-wise now. We must have been on cough syrup when we first did that song. Now the tempo is quicker," he said.

Hutton calls *Harmony* a "softer kind of album," but there is one track that goes away from that formula: the song "Jam," which is the only song on the album that gives Three Dog Night — as a group — a songwriting credit.

"We always liked to put something a little heavier on each album. And that song 'Jam' was actually written on stage at the Whiskey," said Hutton. "It was one of those things where it really was a jam. We didn't have enough songs, really, to fill out the album. If we were playing a place where we had to do two shows, it was one of those things that accidentally started and everybody liked it. We did it a few more times and refined it.

"But if you listen — Heart was big fans of ours — I don't know if it's 'Barracuda' or one of their songs, you'll hear our 'Jam.' They basically took our 'Jam.'"

Harmony remains an album in which Hutton still takes pride.

"I think on every track, you can hear there was really some thought put into it. On all of the tracks, we really went out of our way to get different sounds."

On "An Old Fashioned Love Song" or their cover of the Stevie Wonder song, "Never Dreamed You'd Leave in Summer," the band would leave keyboardist Jimmy Greenspoon to come up with an intro.

"We'd say to Jimmy, 'We'll leave you alone, go into the studio.'

"He would come up with the whole intro himself. Nobody was there, he just said everybody leave, and he would do his famous intros. And it was always good luck. It was like if Jimmy did an intro on something, it was going to be a hit. That's all him."

Hutton said the creativity of Three Dog Night allowed the band to be versatile and attract fans with different tastes. And there's no better example of that than the album *Harmony*.

"If you think about it — and it's not like I'm bragging — there isn't any other group like us that does every kind of music. To be on the rhythm and blues charts, on the easy listening charts, we did a classical album with the London Symphony [Orchestra], and we were on the country charts. We can play a country festival. Country audiences love us. And we did a motorcycle rally with motorcycle guys," said Hutton.

"We just picked songs we liked, and the thing is, the musicians and the singers, we could do anything. We weren't limited. We could actually do any kind of music, even jazz, and from the point of view of whatever genre, I think as good as whatever genre we were in," he said.

Not a law firm

Self-titled
Hamilton, Joe Frank & Reynolds

T hey were so popular in the 1970s that they were called "Playboy's Golden Boys." And Hugh Hefner didn't even know who they were.

At one of Hefner's Playboy Clubs in late 1974, Dan Hamilton, Joe Frank Carollo, and Alan Dennison — Hamilton, Joe Frank & Reynolds — had just signed with Playboy Records, part of Hefner's massive Playboy Enterprises empire. Since 1971 they had been recording with Dunhill Records.

At the time, Hefner's girlfriend, Barbi Benton, wanted to be a singer. So Hef formed a record company for her as well as some other artists at the time, the most notable being the Hudson Brothers and country star Mickey Gilley. And Hamilton, Joe Frank & Reynolds.

"We had this function at one of the Playboy Clubs and I was dating a girl who did makeup for Hef and the magazine, and she was at this function with me," said Joe Frank Carollo. "And the band was over in the corner, and Hef wanted to know who we were. He didn't have a clue. My girlfriend told him, 'Well that's one of your bands.' He was probably thinking, 'Who are these long-haired bunch of hippies? Get them away from my bar.'"

Another time, at a photo shoot at the Playboy Mansion in Los Angeles, the band got to meet Benton.

The Vinyl Dialogues

"Barbi came out to talk to us. And I'm thinking, 'Well this ain't gonna last long.' And she was out there with us maybe for about 10 or 15 minutes, and then I see the curtains pull back from one of Hef's rooms up on the third floor and he opened the window and hollered 'Barbi!' and she said, 'See ya later,'" said Carollo.

Although Carollo got to know Hefner better in later years, that was pretty much the bunny-tail end of Hamilton, Joe Frank & Reynolds' days as "Playboy's Golden Boys."

The path to how they got to the Playboy Mansion that helped establish the band as golden had started a few years earlier in 1971, with the group's debut, self-titled album *Hamilton, Joe Frank & Reynolds*, which featured the hit "Don't Pull Your Love."

In 1966, Hamilton, Carollo, and Tommy Reynolds, performing as an instrumental band called the T-Bones, had a No. 3 hit called "No Matter What Shape (Your Stomach's In)," an instrumental piece based on an Alka-Seltzer commercial.

The three artists left the T-Bones and played clubs around Los Angeles as The Brothers, when Reynolds secured the band an audition with Steve Barri, a record producer at Dunhill Records, purchased by ABC Records in 1967.

"So we went over to the studio — we didn't have any original material, we were just doing cover songs — and they stopped us after a couple of songs and brought out the song 'Don't Pull Your Love.' It was actually recorded by the two guys back on the East Coast who wrote it a year or two before we got ahold of it," said Carollo.

Those two guys were Dennis Lambert and Brian Potter, who would go on to write and produce songs for

66

The Four Tops, Tavares, The Grass Roots, Hall & Oates, and Glen Campbell, including Campbell's 1975 album *Rhinestone Cowboy.*

But in 1971, Lambert and Potter had come to the West Coast as songwriters, not performers. Hamilton, Carollo, and Reynolds had not heard of Lambert and Potter, but when ABC Records officials asked the three musicians to sing "Don't Pull Your Love," the band nailed it.

Joe Frank Carollo as he looked in the mid-1970s, at the height of Hamilton, Joe Frank and Reynolds' popularity.
(Photo courtesy of Joe Frank Carollo)

"They literally signed us that day," said Carollo.

"We liked the song but we thought it was different. We hadn't heard anything like that, but we liked the vocals. That sucker is a bitch to sing because it doesn't leave you a whole lot of room to breathe. So Danny was just worked to death on that thing every time we did it," said Carollo. "But you could tell there was something about the song that you just thought, if it ain't a hit, it's gonna be real close to it."

The band was still called The Brothers — Carollo said he didn't know where that name came from — and the band members had written down a bunch of band names, none of which they liked. So they started kicking around combinations of their last names.

"'Carollo' just didn't seem to fit the way we were doing it," he said. "And I've been called Joe Frank all my life — that was my band back in the 60s, Joe Frank and the Knights — and so we tried that and it sounded good and that's how we ended up with 'Hamilton, Joe Frank & Reynolds.'"

Hamilton, Joe Frank & Reynolds band members by the mid-1970s included, from left, Alan Dennison (who had replaced Tommy Reynolds), Dan Hamilton, Joe Frank Carollo and Johnny Breadu, who was a drummer for the band from 1975-78 and played mainly the live gigs but did not perform on albums.
(Photo courtesy of Joe Frank Carollo)

Hamilton, Joe Frank & Reynolds went into the studio and recorded "Don't Pull Your Love" and then started gathering songs to complete the self-titled debut album. In addition to "Don't Pull Your Love," Lambert and Potter contributed two other songs, "Goin' Down" — written along with Arthur Butler — and "Long Road."

Hamilton and Reynolds teamed up to write "It Takes the Best" and Reynolds added three more songs of his own. Carollo had only one songwriting credit on the album, "Don't Refuse My Love."

"I didn't write. We were all put down as writers, but writing wasn't what I did. We did it as a business thing where we all participated as writers. But I'm a firm believer in that if you write it, you should be the one to make the money off of it," said Carollo.

Once the album was complete, the record company's marketing department took over.

"The first thing they did was send out this little brass-looking thing — a plaque. It was made out of cardboard but it looked like something an attorney would have on his door," said Carollo. "It was stamped 'Hamilton, Joe Frank & Reynolds' and then somebody had written in Magic Marker across the bottom, 'Is not a law firm.'"

When the albums were sent out, they were sent out in gold packing that read, "This record was certified gold the day it left the studio."

Indeed it was.

"I'm not sure exactly what month it came out in, but by July — we were opening for the Carpenters at the Hollywood Bowl — it had gone gold by then because they presented us with a gold record that night," said Carollo.

The single "Don't Pull Your Love" soared to No. 4 on the Billboard Hot 100 chart, while the album itself charted at No. 59.

"Not that we were big-time before, but the T-Bones were a fairly well-known instrumental group. We were big in Japan. So we had had some sort of success already as far as being used to those kinds of things," said Carollo.

But when "Don't Pull Your Love" came out, it actually pushed the band to another level.

"Everything got a little bit better," said Carollo. "I don't know that it created additional pressure, because Danny was a writer and wrote all the time. A lot of people at Motown liked his stuff. He was one of those writers that thought, well, let me try it first and if I can't do it, I'll do something else. He had pretty much written all his life by the time I met him."

Another song on the Hamilton, Joe Frank & Reynolds debut album, "Annabella" — written by Christian Arnold, David Martin and Geoff Morrow — charted at No. 46 on the Billboard Hot 100.

"That ["Annabella"] was one of our favorite songs also, and it came out when most of the guys were coming back from Vietnam. In our shows, we played it all the time, and guys would come up to us and tell us that it was their favorite song," said Carollo.

Although they were considered a Contemporary Top 40 group at the time, Carollo said that the band's shows in that era were totally different than its records.

"Our shows were hard; we liked to boogie, so that's what we did," he said. "But we had to do certain things to make certain records to get ourselves out there. We did all the hits but we also did songs that we liked to play and that we'd been playing for a long time.

"People don't realize it, but by the time 'Don't Pull Your Love' came out, we were already playing it for what seemed like a million times. You wear yourself out playing it sometimes. We were in the studio so much. I didn't even have a radio in my truck. When I got out of the studio after 15 hours in a day, I didn't want to listen to anything. I just wanted to go home and hang out. I don't know if all musicians feel like that or not; I know that's the way I felt about it," said Carollo.

By late 1972, Tommy Reynolds had enough of Hamilton, Joe Frank & Reynolds.

"He wanted to do his material and ABC didn't want to do it at the time. They didn't have any issues doing it down the road, but they didn't want to do it then. And he felt like he needed to do it whenever he needed to do it. So he bailed," said Carollo. Reynolds was replaced by Alan Dennison and the group retained the name Hamilton, Joe Frank & Reynolds.

In the wake of that initial success with the debut album, the band members had talked about becoming a big deal and how to best ride that wave of success.

"But this was a shocker to Danny and I. We had finished up a rehearsal and the next morning, Tommy came to my house — he was a typical long hair, with curly black hair — and he had cut all his hair off. And he had this look like he had taken a step back and didn't know what was going on. And he told me, 'I'm leaving the band.'

"The worst part about it was we were all kind of buddies long before we ever got any hits — we weren't super businessmen — or we would have insisted on something else," said Carollo. "But the way I feel about it, if you don't like what you're doing, get on out, head on."

Reynolds went on to become the lead singer of a band called Shango.

The deal with Playboy Records a few years later, in 1974, was contingent on the band keeping the name "Hamilton, Joe Frank & Reynolds." The band released the single "Fallin' in Love" in the summer of that year. It became the band's only No. 1 hit and was the only No. 1 pop hit in the history of the Playboy Records label before it was taken over by CBS Records. By 1980, the group had disbanded, and in 1993, Hamilton became ill, but nobody seemed to know what was wrong with him.

"I was on the road and had played a New Year's show and then came home, and maybe three or four months later, he got sick," said Carollo. "His wife called me one morning and I went over to the house and we called the ambulance. He stayed in intensive care for a year and then they thought he was doing real good and they sent him home and he had a stroke or a heart attack the next morning and died."

Carollo continues to perform today. He is the front man for "Joe Frank and the World Famous Assistants," a 10-piece blues, R&B, and rock band based in Los Angeles.

But people still remember Hamilton, Joe Frank & Reynolds, and one of their biggest hits, "Don't Pull Your Love," off the self-titled debut album.

"People say to me, 'Man, I heard your song. I was in the elevator.' And I go, 'Yeah, yeah, we get paid for that.' It makes you feel good," said Carollo.

An odd pairing, but a deep friendship

Self-titled
Dave Mason & Cass Elliot

*I*t was a bit of an odd pairing — a one-and-done between friends. But critics loved it; they called it a highly underrated album with awesome songwriting.

Maybe it was a harbinger of more good things to come. But it was never meant to be anything more than it was, according to Dave Mason.

The self-titled album, *Dave Mason & Cass Elliot*, released in 1971 on the Blue Thumb Records label, was mostly a solo project for Mason. He wrote most of the songs and sang most of the leads.

When Traffic — an English rock band formed in 1967 that included Mason, Steve Winwood, Jim Capaldi, and Chris Wood — disbanded in 1969, Mason headed to the United States.

"The fact was, when I first left England and moved to America I was about 22, and the only person I knew in the music scene was Gram Parsons," said Mason. "And I knew some people from Delaney and Bonnie a little bit."

Parsons was a member of The Byrds in the late 1960s, and after that, of The Flying Burrito Brothers. In the summer of 1969, Parsons took Mason to Elliot's house for a visit.

"She had a couple living there that I had known really well in England. So that became a tie-in," said Mason.

After major success with The Mamas and the Papas in the mid-1960s, the band split up, and by the end of 1968 "Mama Cass" had embarked on a solo career. Cass had sung lead on the Mamas and the Papas' single, "Dream a Little Dream of Me," and the success of that hit encouraged Elliot to pursue a solo career.

Mason, the new kid from England, liked Elliot right away and they became friends.

"She was brilliant. She had a great sense of humor — quick, sharp. It was just an interesting time," said Mason.

And the idea for a record featuring the two friends was formed.

"The album came more out of being in that sort of place where a 22-year-old young man could be 7,000 miles away from the country that he grew up in. It became a sort of focal place for me. The album really came out of — it certainly wasn't a great musical pairing like doing Traffic or something like that — it came out of friendship," he said.

At the time, Mason said Elliot was bearing the brunt of jokes about her weight, something that would follow her throughout her career.

"The fact is, and I don't know that most people would remember, but back in the vaudeville days there was a great comedienne named Sophie Tucker. And Cass was that person reincarnated, but she never was portrayed that way in the media. But she could have been. She had a really sharp, cutting sense of humor," said Mason.

For the album, Mason tried to write songs with strong harmonies that would work for both him and Elliot.

The recording sessions were very much like a solo project for Mason. He said he would work out the songs with the band — Bryan Garo on bass, Russ Kunkel on drums, and Paul Harris on keyboards and strings — and the tracks would be mostly done by the time Cass would come in and do her thing.

"I don't think songwriting was really her forte," quipped Mason.

Elliot sang lead on only one song, "Here We Go Again," and shared the songwriting credit with Garo. She also shared songwriting credit with Mason on "Something to Make You Happy," which was also released as a single.

"A lot of the initial response [when the album was released] was that it was a very odd pairing," said Mason. "I think there was a song I wrote which I tried to direct it to be as much of a single as possible, called 'Something to Make You Happy.' And I think it was a minor kind of thing."

To help promote the album, Mason & Elliot did a couple of television appearances and two concerts.

"We did one at the Fillmore East [in Manhattan] and we did one at the Santa Monica Civic Auditorium [in California] and that was it. They were full," said Mason.

And that was indeed it. The album peaked at No. 49 on the Billboard Hot 100 chart in 1971. Although they remained friends after the album's release, Elliot would be gone three short years later, dying of a heart attack in 1974.

"This was just a one-time thing. This was not going to go anywhere. It was never intended to go anywhere. I did it more with her out of friendship," said Mason. "She wanted to do something and she needed something to sort of get her out of that stereotype.

75

"Again, I don't think it was intended to be anything lasting. I'm sure that if the album had been a bigger hit with sales, probably, yeah, we'd have done more stuff," said Mason. "But it sort of came out and then it went away really quick. So there was really no point pursuing it."

Friday nights at Joni's house

The Phlorescent Leech & Eddie
Howard Kaylan and Mark Volman

*T*t was like sitting around the Algonquin Round Table in New York City during the 1920s with the likes of great writers of the time — people like Dorothy Parker and George Kaufman.

Only the writers this time were musicians — people like Stephen Stills, David Crosby, Graham Nash, Jackson Browne, and Joni Mitchell and it was the early 1970s.

And the venue wasn't the historic Algonquin Hotel, in which the greatest writers, critics, and actors of that earlier era gathered to exchange wordplay and witticisms; it was the living room of Joni Mitchell's Laurel Canyon home in California.

There, on any given Friday night, some of the greatest singer-songwriters of their generation would pass around a guitar and play some of the songs they had been working on, songs that hadn't yet been recorded. Songs that would someday be big hits.

And right there along with the musical giants at these "Friday Nights at Joni's House," were Howard Kaylan and Mark Volman of the 1960s' hit-making group, The Turtles, and established stars in their own right.

"It was the early days of an incredible singer-songwriter movement in Los Angeles," said Kaylan. "You were hearing the best songs that these guys had to offer.

So if Graham was working on 'Teach Your Children,' that's what he was playing for everybody. And that's why I felt like such a novice.

"You know, you don't whip out a song like that in front of these peers of yours and then expect to hear anything less from those guys that you're passing the guitar to," said Kaylan. "And for the most part, they didn't disappoint. It was an incredible forum."

But the songs that Kaylan and Volman were playing for their peers in Mitchell's living room were songs they had previously written for what they thought was going to be the next Turtles album.

"I remember exactly the stuff that we were doing," said Kaylan. "In Mark's case, the songs were 'Burn the House' and 'There You Sit Lonely.' In my case, they were 'Strange Girl' and 'I Feel Older Now.'"

Those songs wouldn't end up on an album until 1972, when Volman and Kaylan debuted their first album as a duo, *The Phlorescent Leech & Eddie*.

"I was really just in way over my head," said Kaylan. "Those were cute little album songs. But when you're passing the guitar around and you've got multi-talented human beings like Jackson Browne and Stephen Stills singing their songs, you get to the point where after a while, you don't feel so comfortable breaking out your B-sides."

And yet, as the Friday night jam sessions continued, the competition became more fierce, Kaylan said.

Nash didn't see it the same way.

"I never thought it was competitive, like 'Look at what I wrote.' Stephen and David and Jackson and Joni are ridiculously good songwriters," said Nash. "I didn't feel competitive. I thought it was the joy of the discovery of a new song. We had a lot of music in our lives and that's what we did. We were constantly creating, constantly waking up and dealing with our worlds around us, dealing with our loved ones, dealing with our families and friends and dealing with the world in general."

It was around this time that Nash was working on his debut solo album, *Songs for Beginners*, released in 1971. And these Friday night jam sessions at Mitchell's house were the norm for this creative group.

Like the tunes on *Songs for Beginners*.

"They were songs about my relationship with Joni, my relationship with David and Stephen, my relationship to the political atmosphere in the country at the time," said Nash.

"When we'd go anywhere, we'd take our guitars with us. That's what people did. Everyone carried their guitars around. And, of course, those people — me and David and Stephen and Jackson and Joni — we were very creative. We always had new songs, and the first thing you did is play them for your friends," said Nash.

Sitting around in that group, though, and realizing what he was part of, was not at all lost on Kaylan.

"Everybody kept bringing their best songs, especially Joni and Graham," said Kaylan. "They kept getting better and better."

Mitchell and Nash were in and out of a personal relationship at the time, and although Nash wasn't living with Mitchell then, "his bags were there," Kaylan said.

"What it taught me was that you'd better be damn good," said Kaylan. "You couldn't imitate these people. I guess there was a certain similarity about the tone of the songs because they were all California-inspired. The chord changes were very often Joni Mitchell-inspired with open guitar-tuning changes.

"Everybody, when the guitar hit them, would usually have to retune the guitar for their particular song, just like Joni did," said Kaylan. "Every time she had another song, she had another tuning that would take advantage of that particular song and drone on the chord that would make the most sense to her. She was — and still is — a very smart and instinctual composer."

It was in the context of this setting that Kaylan and Volman continued to evolve. By 1970, Frank Zappa had invited Kaylan and Volman to join a new iteration of The Mothers of Invention. While they were still writing like they were The Turtles, they had hooked up with, and were performing as, Zappa's Mothers of Invention.

"We happened to get sidetracked for two-and-a-half years by Frank Zappa," said Kaylan. "It wasn't our fault; we needed the money." When The Turtles disbanded, they had become embroiled in all kinds of legal proceedings involving the band and its music.

In late 1971, Zappa and The Mothers of Invention were playing a concert at the Rainbow Theatre in London when tragedy struck. During an encore, an audience member jumped onstage and shoved Zappa off the stage and onto the concrete floor of the orchestra pit. The accident put Zappa in a wheelchair for an extended period and essentially put an abrupt end to that iteration of The Mothers of Invention, making Kaylan and Volman unemployed.

Fortunately, they were still under contract to Reprise Records, a label originally founded by Frank Sinatra in 1960, owned by Warner Music Group, and operated through Warner Brothers Records. The Warner corporate types at the company asked Kaylan and Volman what they wanted to do.

"It was Warner's perception that we were comedians," said Kaylan. "And we said, 'Well, that's not the stuff that we have written.' And we played the songs for them [some of the same songs they played at Mitchell's house] and they said, 'Oh, we see, you guys are singer-songwriter guys. That's perfectly wonderful.'"

The studio hired photographer Henry Diltz and art director Gary Burden to give *The Phlorescent Leech & Eddie* album the same treatment that it had given to Crosby, Stills and Nash on their albums.

"We had the matte-finished cover that we wanted, we had all the calligraphy, we had the California look, and the California sound," said Kaylan. "What we didn't have was the California name. You can't call yourselves 'The Phlorescent Leech & Eddie' for God's sake. What the hell does that mean?"

Because of the ongoing legal issues with The Turtles, Zappa had asked Kaylan and Volman to create aliases so that they could be credited for their work on Zappa's 1970 album *Chunga's Revenge*. Kaylan and Volman remembered that they had nicknamed a couple of roadies they knew. One was called "The Phlorescent Leech" because of his colorful wardrobe and mooching ways, and another just looked like an "Eddie," so that's what they called him.

And those are the names they decided they wanted as the credits for their contributions on *Chunga's Revenge*.

Because of Kaylan and Volman's connection to Zappa, Warner Brothers officials thought that "The Phlorescent Leech & Eddie" were household names and that fans would buy the album on that basis.

"And we kept saying, 'Guys, we really don't think that's a very good idea,'" said Kaylan.

So on that first album, Kaylan and Volman are identified by their real names on the cover, right under the made-up and admittedly silly names of "The Phlorescent Leech & Eddie."

Kaylan was "The Phlorescent Leech" and Volman was "Eddie." But that's not how it ended up on that first album.

"It speaks to the fact that even Warner Bothers didn't know enough about who we were, because they printed the pictures in the wrong order," said Kaylan.

When the album came out, the negative of the photo had been flipped.

"And I had to become 'Eddie' instead of 'Phlorescent Leech' and Mark became 'Phlorescent Leech' instead of 'Eddie,'" said Kaylan. "It was just a record company error. And we just figured, why the hell make any waves? What are we going to do, stop the presses now? Let's just release the thing. No one is going to notice anyway. They don't know who the hell we are. And, in fact, they didn't."

One cut from the album, "Feel Older Now," got some radio play and there were a couple of instrumental tracks that worked on FM radio at the time, but for the most part, *The Phlorescent Leech & Eddie* didn't chart.

"We needed badly to cross over into FM because The Turtles had been such an AM hit-making act," said Kaylan. "And the Mothers had been sort of beyond FM radio. We were lucky to have some hit records with Frank Zappa that cracked the Top 10, but normally his stuff was so off-the-beaten-path that radio wouldn't touch it with a 10-foot pole. They were more likely to play our stuff than they were to play Frank's stuff, which is why Frank wanted us in the band in the first place. He wanted to add that little bit of pop sensibility to The Mothers of Invention that they never had before."

Kaylan and Volman went on to do session work for a lot of artists, including John Lennon, Roger McGuinn, David Cassidy, Keith Moon, Alice Cooper, Bruce Springsteen, Duran Duran, and The Ramones. They were also radio stars and appeared in a few movies.

To this day, they still perform as Flo & Eddie, the band's name having been shortened over the years. But they've come back around to their Turtles days, traveling the United States and Canada with the *Happy Together* tour, a gig that features a handful of artists from the 1960s and 1970s that has at various times included the likes of Gary Lewis and the Playboys, The Buckinghams, The Grass Roots, The Association, Micky Dolenz of The Monkees and Chuck Negron of Three Dog Night.

The Turtles' hit single "Happy Together," which supplanted The Beatles' "Penny Lane" at the top of the Billboard Hot 100 charts for three weeks in 1967, remains one of the most recognizable songs of that era of music.

"The great part about being a curmudgeon at my age is that you can't erase history," said the 67-year-old Kaylan. "If 'Happy Together' is indeed one of the top 50 songs of the last century, then I walked heavy on the planet for a minute. I'm not kidding myself; I'm not Neil Armstrong or John Lennon, but it's something. We're only here for a minute on this little dot of a planet. And it's kind of nice to know that you made somebody smile and dance."

Graham Nash signs an autograph for the author during Nash's appearance at Ocean Galleries in Stone Harbor, N.J., in July 2013. Fresh off a Crosby, Stills and Nash tour, Nash was in Stone Harbor to host a collection of his artwork titled *Graham Nash: The Art of Visual Harmony*.
(Photo courtesy of Ocean Galleries, Stone Harbor, N.J.)

84

So much for being on the cover of the *Rolling Stone*

Sloppy Seconds
Dr. Hook & the Medicine Show

The band members of Dr. Hook and the Medicine Show were on the road sometime in 1971 when they got a call from songwriter Shel Silverstein.

"How'd you guys like to get on the cover of *Rolling Stone*?" he asked.

Founded in 1967 by Jann Wenner and Ralph J. Gleason, *Rolling Stone* magazine was highly respected for its political reporting and music coverage. Even in its infancy, being on its cover promised great exposure for a band.

When the band members said, yeah, sure, they'd like to be on the cover of the magazine, Silverstein said, "Well, write this down."

And he proceeded to dictate the lyrics to a song called "The Cover of the *Rolling Stone*." One of the band members wrote the lyrics on the back of his address book.

"We used to travel back then in a nine-passenger station wagon with the whole band and two guitars. We would sit in the back and actually rehearse," said Dennis Locorriere, guitarist and lead singer for Dr. Hook. "And so we worked that song out with me playing acoustic guitar and the rest of the band around a microphone. And

85

we played it that night for the audience and they loved it because of what it said."

The song, which was released as a single in late 1971 and went to No. 6 on the Billboard chart, appeared on Dr. Hook's second album *Sloppy Seconds*, released in 1972.

And what do you know — Silverstein was right. Dr. Hook & the Medicine Show ended up on the cover of *Rolling Stone* on March 29, 1973, but not in a photo. Band members Locorriere, Ray Sawyer, and Billy Francis were depicted in caricature.

And soon thereafter, the band went bankrupt. So much for being on the cover of *Rolling Stone*.

Dennis Locorriere was the lead singer on several songs for Dr. Hook and the Medicine Show when the band recorded *Sloppy Seconds* in 1972. The album featured the single "The Cover of the *Rolling Stone*," written by Shel Silverstein, and the song's popularity did indeed get the band on the cover of *Rolling Stone* magazine. (Photo by Judy Totton)

But more than 40 years later, *Sloppy Seconds* remains one of Dr. Hook's most endearing albums; it turned out to be a better album than folks gave it credit for in the early 1970s.

The original band formed in 1967-68 with members George Cummings, Ray Sawyer, Billy Francis, John "Jay" David, and Locorriere.

"We made a tape for some guy who wanted to be in the music business. His family owned a textile factory but he wanted to be a record producer. He made some tapes with us in a studio. And he really didn't know what to do with them," said Locorriere. "I think he had a line to some label, but they passed. And he passed the tape to someone else. And the guy who wound up with the tape was Ron Haffkine [who eventually became Dr. Hook's producer]."

At the time, Haffkine was the musical director for the 1971 film, *Who is Harry Kellerman and Why Is He Saying Those Terrible Things About Me?* starring Dustin Hoffman, Barbara Harris, Dom DeLuise, and Jack Warden.

The music for the film was written by Shel Silverstein, who by then was also an accomplished poet, author and cartoonist. His work had appeared for years in *Playboy* magazine.

"Ron liked the tape and it was just shit we were playing in bars. But he liked something about my voice and he liked something about the spirit of the band, so he sought us out a little bit and got us an audition," said Locorriere.

Movie studio bigwigs wanted Haffkine to use a popular music act of the time — like Simon and Garfunkel or Crosby, Stills and Nash — artists with the same big-name recognition as the film's star, Dustin Hoffman.

But Haffkine liked the way Dr. Hook sounded, so he put their music in the movie.

"Dustin really liked us, too. He always would have us around the set because he was playing a songwriter and a singer and he didn't know shit about that. So he would come and pick our brains before he would film," said Locorriere.

"I remember one afternoon we were sitting with a couple of guitars in one of the rooms off set playing with Shel, and Dustin was walking through and he was about to film a scene. He stopped, and he said to Ray, 'What do you think about opera?' And Ray went, 'I dunno, it's all right.' And Dustin went, 'OK,' and he walked away. If you watch the movie, there's a scene in there where Barbara Harris says to Dustin, 'What do you think about opera?' And he goes, 'Uh, it's all right.'"

The band stayed on the movie set for its entire production period, often leaving in the evening to play gigs.

"We'd hang around that movie set all day and then we'd go back to the bar we were playing in that night and we'd say, 'Here's a song we recorded for a Dustin Hoffman movie.' And the drunks would go, 'Fuck you, no you didn't.' And then the next morning we'd have to be back on set at 7 a.m. after we had played until 3 in the morning. But it was a killer experience. And it was the beginnings of Dr. Hook," said Locorriere.

The band's self-titled debut album made a bit of a splash, mostly on the strength of the single "Sylvia's Mother," which reached No. 5 on the Billboard chart in 1971.

The combination of "Sylvia's Mother" and the soundtrack from *Harry Kellerman* was enough to attract the attention of Clive Davis, president of CBS Records, who had heard enough of Dr. Hook to request an audience with the band.

"We waited quite a while out in the lobby and people kept coming out and saying, 'Clive will see you soon.' I think the best advantage we had was that none of us were really aware of what a powerful guy Clive was," said Locorriere. "We knew he was the head of the label, but we didn't really know that he had signed so many legendary artists and how powerful he was. So that was an advantage for us because we didn't go in there very nervous. We went in there like the bunch of fuckin' hippies that we were."

According to Locorriere, once inside Davis' office, Francis, the keyboard player, got up on Davis' desk and "danced around a little bit like a goofball" and drummer David "emptied out the wastepaper basket and used it as a drum."

"I think Clive was impressed with the spirit, and you know, we were pretty good with just two guitars. Here's the deal, though: We were doing Shel's material. This was fuckin' stuff that you could recite and get across your point. And we were doing it with some passion and some emotion and stuff like that.

One thing led to another and Clive signed us," said Locorrierre.

Silverstein wrote all 11 songs on *Sloppy Seconds*. And the album benefitted from the experience of the band's first album, which was recorded at A&R Studios in New York City. Haffkine was again the band's producer and he, too, had learned a few things from producing the band's first album.

"When I listen to the first album now — I think most people involved in the album would say the same thing — it suffers from our lack of studio experience," said Locorriere. "We were a bar band, man, and studio stuff is different — much, much different in technique, and we didn't quite have that yet.

"We pulled a lot of it off with passion. We weren't technicians. So there were a few places on the first album where I thought we had really good songs but maybe the arrangements or the way we recorded certain things made them suffer a little bit," he said.

"But it was a good collection of songs and there's some really cool things on there that I know we were just fucking organically bludgeoning our way through. But it really worked."

For *Sloppy Seconds* the band relocated to the CBS studio in San Francisco, on Folsom Street. Also recording in the studio at that time in 1971 were Barbra Streisand, Paul Simon (on his self-titled first solo album, released in January 1972), and the group Santana.

And there was even more creative magic going on right next door, although Locorriere and the other band members didn't realize it at the time.

"There was a doorway with a little narrow hallway and a stairway going up with a little brass plaque on the wall that read 'American Zoetrope,' which turned out to be Francis Ford Coppola's studio," said Locorriere. "He was probably cutting *The Godfather* in there at about that time. And we didn't know it. A little tiny hallway with a staircase. We never even went in there and we were right next door."

Because the band members and Haffkine knew their way around a studio a little better by the time they worked on their second album, they decided to augment their sound.

"We really didn't augment on the first record. We did use a few outside musicians on *Sloppy Seconds*. And you know I look at the credits today and I'm embarrassed to say that they're not even credited. But it made for a little more solid sound. It sounded more like we knew what we were doing," said Locorriere.

Sloppy Seconds is bracketed by two strong, yet diverse tunes, "Freakin' at the Freaker's Ball" to start, and "The Cover of the *Rolling Stone*" to close. Those are the two songs on the album that made most of the headlines, but there are nine other songs that Locorriere said could have and should have gotten more attention.

"It opens with 'Freakin' at the Freaker's Ball' and the listener has no idea what this band sounds like, even by the end of that song. Then there is a whole bunch of songs like 'Carry Me, Carrie' and 'The Things I Didn't Say' and all these heartfelt songs. Then it ends with 'The Cover of the *Rolling Stone*.' It's like we opened and closed with all this ridiculous shit, and then there's all this stuff in the middle. And those are the songs that I really want to play nowadays. I really like to play the songs that make people go, 'Oh, I didn't think you'd sing that one.' I really do, because when I go see an artist, that's what I like."

The album cover of *Sloppy Seconds* features just the heads of the band members — Locorriere, Sawyer (with his trademark eyepatch), Francis, Cummings, David, Rik Elswit, and Jance Garfat. They're all cracking up — and maybe, just maybe — a little high.

The picture was shot by famed rockstar photographer Jim Marshall, who by then was already renowned for photographing Jimi Hendrix setting his

guitar on fire at the Monterey Pop Festival in 1967, and
for taking the cover shot for the 1969 album *Johnny Cash
at San Quentin.*

"Jim Marshall was a brilliant photographer. We
went to his house in California, out in his backyard, and
he was a cantankerous son of a bitch, man. He really had
no patience. He would snap at us and bark at us," said
Locorriere. "And one of the reasons we were laughing like
that was because he was angry at us and treating us like a
bunch of kids. And I guess we were acting like a bunch of
kids. But he was jamming us in like that [all into one
shot] and we were just laughing our asses off. And he was
yelling at us the whole time, and not even in kind of a
friendly way. He was like, 'C'mon! I'm not gonna fuckin'
do this all day!' And the shot he got was us reacting to
'What the fuck is the matter with this guy?'"

The photo on the back cover of *Sloppy Seconds* is
of the band in Sausalito, California, where Silverstein
moored a houseboat. Band members were walking on the
pier singing "Freaker's Ball" when the photograph was
taken.

"Poor Rik doesn't wind up in the shot because he
was far left and they [studio officials] liked the shot, so
they thought, 'So what? The rest of you guys look good,'"
said Locorriere.

Locorriere believes that the success of the single
"The Cover of the *Rolling Stone*," eventually did force the
magazine's hand to the point where the editors had to put
Dr. Hook on the cover.

"We were a bunch of fuckin' rag-tags, man. We
were the underdogs. And that's why that song worked for
us," said Locorriere. "But they played it on the radio until
the magazine, really, almost had no choice. It came out
near the end of 1971 and it got played pretty well. And

92

the song was in the magazine's year-end wrap-up article. They gave us an 'honorable mention.' And then it was forgotten."

In what turned out to be prophetic, Dr. Hook recorded one more album for CBS, *Belly Up* in 1973, before going belly up. The turn of fortune coincided with Davis' departure from CBS.

"And as soon as Clive lost his gig, so did we," said Locorriere. "The next guy who took over CBS Records was actually a guy that used to be the head of CBS Television and he didn't know anything other than being the head of CBS Something. He was just kind of propping the door open. And then they did a big overhaul and somebody said, 'Who signed these fuckin' hippies?' and we were gone. We didn't have that champion in Clive anymore."

Dr. Hook signed with Capitol Records in 1975 and the band's first album on the new label was wryly titled *Bankrupt*. Things had changed from the early days. But more importantly for its future success, the band also began to reinvent itself.

"And we kind of wormed our way back. Then we all got haircuts and we leaned a lot on my vocals and we started to look for more mainstream material — and we started to have hits," said Locorriere, referring to two songs that each hit No. 6 on the charts in 1978, "Sharing the Night Together" and "When You're in Love with a Beautiful Woman," both from the album *Pleasure and Pain.*

"The band was no longer as interesting on a record as we were live, but we were feeding our families. It was a tradeoff. It's like the Donner Party. We didn't want to have to eat people, but we did what we had to do to survive," said Locorriere.

"In the early days, we really had a lot of fun because everything wasn't riding on it yet. It could go nowhere but up," he said. "One of the interesting things about those days is that it was all or nothing, but we didn't have so much of everything that it was a big loss.

"We didn't have the houses yet and shit like that. We had a house. We lived in Sausalito in a house. We couldn't even afford a phone, so we had a pay phone put in the house. We had a phone booth in our living room. If you were gonna make a phone call, you had to use your own fuckin' change. And we always thought that was very fitting that the band that had a number one record ["Sylvia's Mother"] had a pay phone in their fuckin' living room.

"They were more communal days. As the band went on and we had more hits and radio records and we started doing international tours, then you need now to have more radio hits, you need to stay on stop. The scale of everything goes up. You're living better and you're trying to keep that for your families, especially after you've gone broke once," he said.

"So then you go commercial and it changes the complexion of stuff, man. It gets a little more serious. We went from a sign that said 'Dr. Hook & the Medicine Show, Cold Beer and Go-Go Girls' to 'Dr. Hook, Inc.' with 30 people on staff. In the beginning we would play a bar and we'd get the money at the end of the week, we'd buy groceries and we'd split the rest of it up so we could all have five or 10 fuckin' bucks. You got nothing to protect yet. What fucks everything up is once you have something to protect."

94

Even now, Locorriere believes *Sloppy Seconds* was a better album than it was given credit for at the time of its release. And even though later albums had more commercial success, something was missing from those albums.

"I think some of our biggest records were a lot less creative and imaginative than we were being back in those early days. I think they were calculated and we gambled right," he said. "I went from being the guy in the long bathrobe and the long hair and beard with bits of my lunch in it to the guy wearing eyeliner and singing fuckin' 'Sexy Eyes.' These days I'm proud of that because I think that's a helluva thing for a guy to be able to do. To roll with the times like that.

"But I didn't sell the band out. We all knew what we were doing. We wanted to eat. And I could sing that stuff.

"And then we started using Muscle Shoals Rhythm Section on 'When You're in Love with a Beautiful Woman.' Those are the same guys who played on Aretha Franklin records and Bob Seger records and Paul Simon records.

"Dr. Hook was still a great road band, but we still could not go in a studio and knock out an album. It would take the band forever.

"With *Sloppy Seconds*, that was the band every day in the studio coming up with ideas. That's what it was," he said.

Riding nostalgia all the way to stardom

Innerview
The Statler Brothers

A simple day of unwinding and rocking on a front porch ended with what would become a career-building song for The Statler Brothers.

Brothers Don and Harold Reid — along with Phil Balsley and Lew DeWitt — had formed a country music quartet in the mid-1950s. By 1964, the group had established itself enough to back up country legend Johnny Cash.

The Statler Brothers, from left, Harold Reid, Don Reid, Phil Balsley and Lew DeWitt, perform with Johnny Cash, far left, in the late 1960s. The Statler Brothers opened for Cash for more than eight years, from the mid-1960s through the early 1970s. (Photo courtesy of The Statler Brothers)

In the early days of touring with Johnny Cash in 1964, The Statler Brothers pose backstage with The Man in Black before a performance.
(Photo courtesy of The Statler Brothers)

For the next eight and a half years, they would be part of Cash's traveling troupe, as well as regulars on Cash's ABC hit television show, *The Johnny Cash Show*, which ran from 1969 to 1971.

The Statlers' first hit, "Flowers on the Wall," released in 1965, rose all the way to No. 2 on the Billboard Hot Country Singles chart. But by the early 1970s, it was time for The Statler Brothers to venture out on their own. They had gained invaluable experience in the country music business during the group's tenure with Cash. They had tasted success, but there was still more to explore.

With Cash's blessing, of course.

"It was a big transition for us because we had been with John since 1964 and we had a hit record with 'Flowers on the Wall.' But we didn't leave the troupe. We could have at that point gone out and taken advantage of that but we wanted to hang around with him [Cash] and pay him back for what he'd done for us," said Don Reid.

"But by the early '70s we had done the ABC *Johnny Cash Show* with him and we felt like it was time to move on. We were getting all kinds of dates on our own. In 1970-71, we were doing all of John's concert dates plus we were doing our own. We were working all the time. There was never a weekend off," said Reid.

And Cash agreed.

"We had sensed in conversations that he [Cash] realized what we were doing, realized where we were and that it was time to take advantage of it. It was kind of like leaving home. You're losing some comfort there, but at the same time we were excited about it and wanted to do it.

"John said, 'Yeah, I know what you're doing. I don't blame you. Go for it.' So we left," said Reid.

And they continued to write original songs. That was how Don and Harold Reid ended up on Harold's front porch in Staunton, Virginia, one day in the early 1970s. They started with a simple idea: Make a list of things they remembered from their childhoods.

They wrote and wrote, and the list grew and grew. They started in the 1950s, including memories like Saturday morning serials, flat top haircuts, sock hops, movie stars on Dixie Cup tops, knickers, pedal pushers, duck-tail hair, Cracker Jack prizes, boatneck shirts, Ovaltine, Roy Rogers, Charles Atlas, and knock-knock jokes.

"We started writing the song and we wrote pages full of stuff. I remember so well we were sitting on Harold's front porch one early spring day and we're writing and when we got through, we said we have to cut this down to where it's a song. We had to get about four verses out of it. And we threw some verses away. We just were having fun with all the things we could remember from our childhoods," said Don.

The Statler Brothers' "Do You Remember These" would become a mega-hit, and would anchor the 1972 album *Innerview*. Not only that, it would be the first of the "nostalgia songs" that the Statlers would make famous.

And the Reid brothers sensed that on that day, on Harold Reid's front porch, they had created something special.

"We went in and recorded it and we thought right away that we had a hit there," said Don. "Sometimes you can feel it, right in the middle of when you're writing it. You say, 'Man, this is gonna be good.' Or you might say, 'This needs some more work. It's laying kind of flat.'

"But the advantage of writing with my brother is that Harold and I have always been very close. We grew up together. So we've always had this thing. We've worked together on stage, we've worked together in the [recording] sessions, on TV. And we're very honest with each other. When we're sitting and writing a song together and one of us will come up with a line, he and I have no problems with each other saying, 'Ah, that's not very good, we can do better than that.' With some people you worry about hurting their feelings. But we never considered that. We just say, 'Nah, it's no good,' and then keep on going. So it's a great advantage writing with someone that close to you."

By the early 1970s the Statlers had a substantial library of original material that had yet to be recorded. But when it came time to put together the *Innerview* album, only half of the songs were original Statler Brothers songs. The other half of the album included songs written and previously recorded by other artists.

Among those were "I'd Rather be Sorry," written by Kris Kristofferson and recorded by Ray Price; "Got Leavin' on Her Mind," written by Jack H. Clement and recorded by Charlie Pride; "Take Me Home, Country Roads," co-written and recorded by John Denver; "She

Thinks I Still Care," a No. 1 hit for George Jones a decade earlier in 1962; "Every Day Will Be Sunday By and By," written by Bob Miller and recorded by The Blackwell Brothers; and "Never Ending Song of Love," written and recorded by Delaney and Bonnie.

"We did the covers because we felt that it was sort of like insurance on an album. We were still early in our career and we were still new to a lot of people," said Don.

"We had what we called a good original song, 'Do You Remember These,' which was a hit. But when people pick up an album and see The Statler Brothers and then they see that we've also got 'I'd Rather Be Sorry,' 'Take Me Home, Country Roads,' and 'She Thinks I Still Care,' people think, 'Oh, I'd like to hear their version of it.' Because those songs, just the titles themselves, carried some weight. So we kind of thought of it as insurance for albums, and that's why we were very open to including cover songs in those days. People like to see familiarity when they pick up a new album," he said.

Of The Statler Brothers' originals, Don and Harold wrote the song "Daddy" for the *Innerview* album, which, according to Don, was just a story about an everyday man who had never become famous. Although it isn't primarily about the Reids' own father, Sidney, who had died in 1967, "There was some of him in that song," admitted Don.

"Do You Remember These" was the only single released from *Innerview*, but if another single had been released, Don said, "Never Ending Love" by Delaney and Bonnie would have been his choice.

"Sometimes we went with two singles [off an album], sometimes we didn't. If we had gone with two, that would have been my vote because I think it really had a lot of radio feel to it. I think it would have been good," recalled Don.

The name of the album, *Innerview*, was intentionally designed to be a play on words, according to Don.

"It was an inner view of The Statler Brothers and who we were," he said. "Because you see on the album a song 'Every Day Will Be Sunday By and By,' which is an old southern gospel song that The Blackwood Brothers recorded back in the 1950s when we were growing up. And we were singing it in church when we were kids. That was very much a part of who we were and what we were, so that song is on that album. It was an album about looking inside of who we were."

Innerview, released in 1972, was the third studio album of the 16 albums recorded by The Statler Brothers in the 1970s on the Mercury Records label. The first album for the label was *Bed of Rose's*, released in 1970. The title track was written by Harold Reid, and was about a young man who takes up with a prostitute twice his age, much to the chagrin of the churchgoing townspeople. It became a Top 10 single and propelled the album to No. 5 on the country charts.

But it was the single "Do You Remember These" from the *Innerview* album that took the Statlers to country music superstardom.

"People would stop us on the street, or at home, or if we were out on tour, and say, 'I remember everything you all mentioned in that song.' That was a big thing. And then they'd want to tell you a story about sock hops or something else. That song really triggered people's memories," said Don.

"I think people can tell if you're just writing for money, or writing for whatever the trend is or if you are writing from your heart. And that's what we were doing — we were following our hearts and writing about the things we knew about. I think people do sense that, absolutely."

It was a career-building song.

"It sort of identified us as to who we were. It set us up for our next hit, 'Class of '57,' which was a continuation of the nostalgia thing. And that song was even bigger. It took us to another level, without a doubt."

From there, it was only upward for The Statler Brothers. Don Reid sang lead, Harold Reid sang bass, Phil Balsley sang baritone, and Lew DeWitt sang tenor. Health issues forced DeWitt to leave the group in 1983, and he died in 1990 from complications of Crohn's disease. He was replaced by Jimmy Fortune, who remained with the group until it disbanded, and they retired from active touring and recording in 2002.

The Statlers garnered numerous awards over the course of their careers, and the group was inducted into the Gospel Hall of Fame in 2007 and the Country Music Hall of Fame in 2008. But it was those early days with Johnny Cash, according to Don Reid, that kept the group grounded and able to handle its success with grace and appreciation.

"We got our music business education from John. He was a great friend and he was a great artist. He had his demons and he had his problems and we were there, close with him, practically living with him for eight-and-a-half years. We learned a lot of the things not to do, honestly. And he would have been the first to have laughed and told you that was true when he was having his bad periods," said Don.

"So we watched and we learned some great things to do, how to do things. You can't find a better songwriter than Johnny Cash. When he was right, buddy he was good, and I learned a lot from him."

In fact, it was Cash who gave Don Reid the best songwriting advice he ever received.

"We were writing a song one day and I was having trouble with some wording and I asked him about it. And he said, 'Hey, just always remember, the best way to say anything is to just say it.' That's always been my favorite advice ever. Sometimes you just cut through all the roses and all the B.S. and just put down what's in your mind and in your heart. Don't worry about everything else; just say it. And that's how he was, with that hard-edged way of writing. And I think it was always good advice."

The Statlers were fortunate that even as young men, they realized the opportunity they were being given by Johnny Cash.

"We didn't take any of that for granted. Every day, we realized, 'Hey, we're in a special place and we can absorb this.' We could grow from it. And we did. We were aware of it. I don't know now how or why we were, but we were aware of it. We tried to take advantage of all the situations we had and what we were surrounded with," said Don.

As far as the *Innerview* album, Don Reid maintains that more than 40 years later, it still resonates, both from a career standpoint and with fans.

"To me, it stacks up pretty good. I think it's really solid. It's a picture of who we were and who we are," he said. "We were always looking for good songs. We were very song-conscious. We never just filled in an album with, 'Hey, we need another song,' and just threw one in there. We always were very lyric-conscious, something that we could do, that we could sell, that we could arrange, and I think we always had good songs.

"The whole album is full of good songs, whether we wrote them or somebody else did. They're darn good songs, I think, and we always tried to fill an album with good material," he said.

The 'magic side' of the record

Abandoned Luncheonette
𝓗𝓪𝓵𝓵 & 𝓞𝓪𝓽𝓮𝓼

Daryl Hall and John Oates had a choice to make. In November 1972 they had released their debut album, *Whole Oats*, for Atlantic Records but with little acclaim. A few months later, in early 1973, record producer Kenny Gamble approached the duo and wanted them to work at Philadelphia International Records, as songwriters and recording artists.

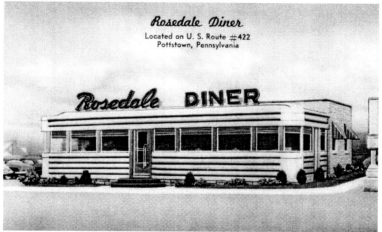

This is a postcard of the Rosedale Diner, which was on High Street in Pottstown, Pennsylvania, in the 1960s, before it closed, was moved out of town, and became the "Abandoned Luncheonette." It was owned by Talmadge W. "Bill" Faulk, who is credited on the back of the *Abandoned Luncheonette* album as: "Luncheonette courtesy of The Man on Route 724." (Photo courtesy of Larry Cultrera)

Philadelphia was a happening place in those days, thanks to Gamble and fellow producer Leon Huff. It was early in the creation of what is now known as "Philly soul" — sometimes called "the Philadelphia Sound" — soul music that included funk influences and arrangements heavy on strings and horns.

Their difficult choice: Hall and Oates could stay in Philly and work for Gamble and Huff at Philly International, or they could move to New York and make their second album for Atlantic Records.

"The idea was that we had all these obvious Philly influences — it was our baby food; it's what we are," said Hall. "John had a real grounding in the alternative Philly sound, which was very folksy. We wanted to combine two elements — my gospel R&B experiences and John's folk experiences — and make a hybrid record that was sort of indicative of the sound of Philadelphia."

That's what *Abandoned Luncheonette* was all about. And Hall and Oates chose to move to New York to make the album.

More than 40 years since the release of that album, both Hall and Oates are as proud of it now as they were then. Oates doesn't hesitate to call it his favorite Hall & Oates album.

"It's a special album. It was a perfect storm of creativity for us," said Oates. "It was the right producer [Arif Mardin] in the right studio with the right musicians and the right songs all at the same time. That seldom happens, but you hope it does. Fortunately for us, it happened on our second album."

The benefit of hindsight over the last 40 years has done little to change the belief of either artist that the primary reasons *Abandoned Luncheonette* has stood the test of time is that the songwriting was just that good, and the musicians were just that talented.

106

"It was very much a Daryl and John album," said Hall. "We were really clicking as a creative team in those days. There are a lot of great John Oates moments on that album that still really impress me.

"But things sort of evolved after that. I took on more and the balance shifted of what our functions were within Hall & Oates. But in those days, we were just kids and we were just trying."

Oates said that, now, the songs sound innocent and they sound simple.

"But the bottom line is, they still sound good," he said. "And that's all that really matters. Whether it sounds like another person wrote them — which to me they kind of do — that really doesn't matter," said Oates. "What matters is that I can still play them and people still like them and they still sound good.

"And that's the mark of a song — to stand the test of time. It's the ultimate goal for a songwriter. It's what you hope for, the benchmark you go for every time you write a song. You don't always attain it, but that's your goal," he said.

Hall said that side one of *Abandoned Luncheonette* is the "magic" side. It includes one Hall-penned tune, "When the Morning Comes;" three by Oates, "Had I Known You Better Then," "Las Vegas Turnaround," and "I'm Just a Kid (Don't Make Me Feel Like a Man);" and the co-written hit, "She's Gone," which was only moderately successful when it was first released as a single in 1974. But it climbed to No. 7 on the charts when a remixed version was re-released in 1976, after the duo had moved to RCA Records and scored big with the hit single, "Sara Smile."

"On Side One, there's not a note on that body of work that isn't just right," said Hall, citing the environment in the Atlantic Records studio in which *Abandoned Luncheonette* was recorded.

"Aretha Franklin was walking in and out. Bob Dylan was walking in and out. Dr. John was nodding in and out. All the studio musicians were in the room regularly, and that's the environment we cut this music in."

The musicians who worked on *Abandoned Luncheonette* included Chris Bond on electric guitar, acoustic guitar, and synthesizer; Hugh McCracken on electric guitar; Steve "Fontz" Gelfand on bass; Bernard Purdie on drums; Ralph MacDonald on percussion; Joe Farrell on oboe and tenor sax; Jerry Ricks on acoustic guitar; Rick Marotta on drums and percussion; Steven Moore on drums, percussion, and vocals; Gordon Edwards on bass; Pancho Morales on conga; Pat Rebillot on organ; Richard Tee on piano; Gloria Agostini on harp; John Blar on Vitar electric violin; Marvin Stamm on flugelhorn; Larry Packer on fiddle; Marc Horowitz on banjo; and Arif Mardin on bass, vocals, horn, and string arrangements.

"We were thrilled to be on Atlantic Records and we were thrilled that Arif was going to surround us with the absolute creme de la creme of musicians on every level," said Oates. "If you look at the players on this album, you're talking about people like Joe Farrell, one of the greatest jazz saxophonists of all time; you're talking about Bernard Purdie, one of the greatest R&B drummers of all time. Everybody, the players on this record, are just ridiculous. And Daryl and I were entering a place where we were at the top of our game as songwriters. Everything was right."

Side Two of the album has a different vibe, though, according to Hall. It features the influence of Bond, a guitarist for Hall & Oates who wanted to be a producer. As the project progressed, Bond got more and more involved.

"Whenever you hear something that sounds Beatles-esque — when it's obvious Beatles-esque — can trace that back to Chris Bond," said Hall, who added that Bond is "an outrageously talented guitar player."

"I have become a Beatles fan over the years, but back in 1972-73, I was not a gigantic Beatles fan. So to have that stuff as part of our arrangement was not really consistent with the character of what I wanted to do," said Hall.

"In those days, [Bond] was obsessed with The Beatles and I was not. So side two, if I could change anything, I'd just get rid of all that crap and let the songs be the songs." And side two of the album features the eponymous title track, "Abandoned Luncheonette," written by Hall, the theme of which he said, is that only the strong survive.

Hall said the song is written about people who give up, and people who do something with their lives.

"It could have been called 'Abandoned Lives.' It was about people who gave up and wound up in the same place they started in, only not even as good.

"If you look at the lyrics of that song, even as a kid I knew that only the strong survive," said Hall. "I've used that theme — the strong move on and the weak give up and stay — to say that the idea is that you have to make something of your life. You have to go for it. And I guess life has proven me right about that — at least in my case."

When it came time to come up with a name for the album, Hall suggested it be called *Abandoned Luncheonette*. He remembered that there was an abandoned diner near his grandmother's house outside of Pottstown, Pennsylvania.

"So I said, 'This place is all falling down. Let's take a photographer up there and take a picture.' So that's what we did," said Hall. "The cops came and threw us out because we were trespassing on somebody's property. But we did manage to get the pictures that we wanted, and that's where the whole idea and the concept of the album cover came from. It really didn't come from the song; it was just coincidental."

The "Abandoned Luncheonette" as it looked in 1982, nine years after the release of the album of the same name by Daryl Hall and John Oates. The final resting place of the rundown diner was in a wooded area just off Route 724 in Kenilworth, Pennsylvania.
(Photo courtesy of Larry Cultrera)

One of those pictures did indeed become the album cover — the picture of the dilapidated diner — and another photo, of Hall and Oates sitting inside the diner, graces the back cover of the album.

"It was one of those things that just worked. It speaks as a piece of art, really. I kind of wish album covers were still around," said Oates. The photographer was Oates' girlfriend at the time, Barbara Wilson, who is credited as "B. Wilson" on the inside album sleeve. She was a student at the Philadelphia College of Art, which would eventually merge with the Philadelphia College of

Performing Arts in 1985 to create what is now known as the University of the Arts in Philadelphia.

After the album became a hit, there was a time in the mid- to late-1970s when fans and curiosity seekers would search out the rundown diner that sat in a wooded area just off Route 724 in Kenilworth, Pennsylvania. Souvenir hunters eventually picked apart the already long-ignored structure, which at one time had been called the Rosedale Diner when it was located on High Street in Pottstown.

After it went out of business, the structure was moved outside of town and essentially left to die in East Coventry Township, eventually becoming the "Abandoned Luncheonette."

Hall still has some pieces of the old diner. "Fans came from all over the world. And unfortunately for the guy who owned it, they basically destroyed it; they ripped it apart tile by tile, piece by piece. Somebody gave me some tiles from it over the years. I've gotten little pieces of it from fans. That's really an unusual story," Hall reminisced.

That album essentially put the local musicians — Hall from Pottstown and a graduate of Owen J. Roberts High School, and Oates, from North Wales and a graduate of North Penn High School — on the road to stardom.

Both artists recall the significant role the diner played in the marketing of the album.

Hall — born Daryl Hohl — remembers his parents taking him to the Rosedale Diner as a young boy. The diner's owner, Talmadge W. "Bill" Faulk, closed it in the mid-1960s, and had the structure moved a few miles outside of Pottstown to some land he owned along Route 724. And its new resting place was right near where Daryl Hall's grandmother lived.

Bill Faulk is credited on the inside cover sleeve: "Luncheonette courtesy of The Man on Route 724."

This is an interior shot of the "Abandoned Luncheonette" in 1982. The structure had been picked over by souvenir hunters by then and was even more dilapidated than it was in 1973 when it was featured on the Hall & Oates album cover. (Photo courtesy of Larry Cultrera)

Another song from *Abandoned Luncheonette* involved the Oates-penned song, "Las Vegas Turnaround." It wouldn't become a big hit for the duo, but it did lay the groundwork for what would become another Hall & Oates hit.

According to Oates, he had met a flight attendant — they were called "stewardesses" back then — and a girlfriend on the street in New York, and struck up a conversation with the two of them. The flight attendant's name was Sara, and during their discussion, Sara mentioned that she and her friend were getting ready to do a "Las Vegas turnaround."

"I didn't know what they were talking about," said Oates. "They told me, 'Oh, that's where we take a group of gamblers out to Las Vegas and then we just turn around and come back.' That's the type of thing a songwriter hears and turns into a song."

Oates would eventually introduce Sara Allen to Hall, the two of them would start a relationship that lasted more than 30 years, and she would become the inspiration for the song "Sara Smile," the duo's first Top 10 hit, reaching all the way to No. 4 in 1976.

Unlike Oates, Hall won't go so far as to say that *Abandoned Luncheonette* is his favorite Hall & Oates album.

"You can never look into the future, but I was proud of it at the time," said Hall. "Would I have known that we'd be talking about it 40 years later? No, but I had the feeling it was going to be around for a while.

"But it was one of my favorite experiences, I'll say that," he said. "I guess I would equate that with a favorite album."

O'Connelly Corners in just 48 seconds

The Captain and Me
The Doobie Brothers

On Side Two of The Doobie Brothers' 1973 album, *The Captain and Me*, there's a 48-second guitar instrumental track titled "Busted Down Around O'Connelly Corners." The song is listed on the record between "Evil Woman" and "Ukiah," but one has to actually look at the record itself to know that the song is there. It's not listed on the back of the album cover.

"That was a tune that a friend of mine had written," said original Doobies' guitarist Patrick Simmons. "There's actually more to it than what's on the record."

Before he joined The Doobie Brothers, Simmons hung out in southern California perfecting his craft. After playing club gigs, Simmons and his friends would oftentimes head to Mike O'Connelly's place in an apartment building on Main Street in Los Gatos, California, to relax, play their guitars, and sing.

"We'd sit around and somebody would play a song and the rest of us would sing along. It was kind of like a poor man's Bluebird Cafe," said Simmons, referring to the famous club in Nashville, Tennessee that attracts singers and songwriters to its intimate setting.

They'd hang out at Mike's place so much that they started referring to the apartment building as "O'Connelly Corners."

"One time Mike had walked outside the apartment building and was getting in the car to go someplace," said Simmons. "He had a joint on him or something, and the cops arrested him." And that was the inspiration for the song "Busted Down Around O'Connelly Corners," written by James Earl Luft.

By the time The Doobie Brothers were recording their third studio album, *The Captain and Me*, the record's producer, Ted Templeman, had become a big fan of Simmons' "traditional ragtime guitar picking."

"So Ted said, 'Hey, Pat, you got something you can put on this album,'" recalled Simmons.

And that's how the first 48 seconds of "Busted Down Around O'Connelly Corners" made it onto side two of *The Captain and Me*.

Between recording their second and third albums, The Doobie Brothers had been on a roll. The band's 1971 debut studio album, self-titled *The Doobie Brothers*, wasn't met with great success, selling maybe 40,000 to 50,000 copies, according to Simmons.

But their second album, *Toulouse Street*, released in 1972, was the band's entry into the national marketplace, and secured The Doobie Brothers their first major national tour, opening for Marc Bolan and T. Rex.

"That was a big moment for us because we were sort of the new kids on the block and that introduced us to a much larger audience," said Simmons. "We had these hits off *Toulouse Street* — 'Listen to the Music,' 'Jesus Is Just Alright,' and 'Rockin' Down the Highway,' — that got played quite a lot."

Simmons and fellow original Doobie Brothers member Tom Johnston had each written quite a few songs, even prior to recording *Toulouse Street* that didn't make the cut for that album, so they were looking forward to getting back into the studio and recording their third album in late 1972.

116

One song that didn't make the cut for *Toulouse Street* was "Long Train Runnin'," a song that the band had played many times onstage that had no real structure to it. It didn't have any lyrics, either.

"Tommy would get up and just kind of scat through it and sing the blues. He'd take a guitar solo and I'd take a guitar solo and we'd just play it out as a funky groove, sort of a Latin funk. And we'd just sort of jam along," said Simmons.

Once again, producer Templeman offered direction. He suggested that words be put to the jam before the band recorded it at what was then called Amigo Studios, a division of Warner Brothers, in North Hollywood, California.

"The solo itself became a harmonica solo, which was kind of cool," said Simmons. "We didn't have that in the original arrangement, which was a lot of guitars.

"I sat in with Ted for a while, while the guys were working on the track — bass drums, guitars — and then I went into an adjacent space in between the walls and I took my acoustic guitar and I started playing around," said Simmons. "And I came up with my part while the guys were cutting the track. As soon as the track was cut, I went in and laid down my track."

Simmons said the song was kind of a straight-ahead, blues-rock tune.

"It was something we could all sink our teeth into," he said. "We had been playing the tune for the better part of two-and-a-half to three years on and off in our club sets, but we really didn't have this creative arrangement. It really came to life not only as a studio track, but as a live tune. We got something really cool out of it, and to this day, we still play the track. It's the highlight of our set, I think."

"Long Train Runnin'" peaked at No. 8 on the Billboard Hot 100 in 1973.

Another song from *The Captain and Me* that
ended up as a Top 20 single — reaching No. 15 — was
"China Grove."

According to Johnston, the band was touring in a
Winnebago in 1972 and had just started to get national
recognition. While driving through Texas, they passed a
road sign that read "China Grove."

"But I didn't see it, or if I did, I didn't remember
it," said Johnston. "We were headed into San Antonio at
the time and my thinking was that I saw the name 'China
Grove' without having it really register in the frontal
lobe."

Johnston wrote the song in early 1973 based on a
piano lick by Billy Payne.

"And I made up all these ridiculous lyrics about
sheriffs and samurai swords and all that kind of stuff,"
said Johnston. "But at that time, I still believed it was a
completely fictional place."

In 1975, Johnston got into a cab in Houston,
Texas. He and the cabdriver struck up a conversation, and
once the cabbie realized that Johnston was a member of
The Doobie Brothers, he posed a question.

"He said, 'What made you write a song about that
little old town, China Grove?' I said, 'What town, China
Grove? I've never heard of a town called China Grove.'
He said, 'Yeah, it's right down there, like the song says,
right outside San Antonio.' That blew me out of the water,
it really did," said Johnston. "That was a trip. I thought he
was pulling my chain."

Although none of the other songs on *The Captain
and Me* charted as singles, the hidden gem may be the
Simmons-penned song, "South City Midnight Lady."

Simmons said that the band had a sense that some
songs – like "Long Train Runnin'" and "China Grove" —
had commercial appeal and the potential to get wide play
on the radio. But "South City Midnight Lady" was what

118

the band members called an "album track," and not a commercial type of song.

The song is about living in Los Gatos, California, which is at the southern end of the bay area. Simmons was living with his girlfriend at the time and was trying to write a romantic song.

"I don't necessarily look at it as that personal, but it probably is," said Simmons. "I was up all night writing that song. By 4 or 5 in the morning, I was pretty much finished with the song and I had the arrangement idea pretty much together.

"It was interesting because a friend of mine showed up in the morning and knocked on my door. It was pretty early, around 7 a.m., and I was surprised that he showed up that early. And he was surprised I was awake that early, but in fact I had been up all night," said Simmons.

"I remember playing the song for him and him liking it and then I think I went to bed. I can't even remember if my girlfriend liked the song, but I'm sure she thought it was OK."

Album covers of that era were oftentimes considered works of art that complemented the songs on the album, and *The Captain and Me* is no different.

Simmons said the band members used to sit around and conceptualize ideas for album covers. Doobie Brothers drummer John Hartman was always an idea guy, according to Simmons.

"He was a little eccentric and he liked to come up with crazy concepts, musically and visually," said Simmons. "We were brainstorming one time — we used to sit around and smoke ... something ... well into the night.

"We had several ideas floating around and we came up with the idea of the coach and the outfits — sort of the Old English or early American formal wear, that really didn't mean anything. We just thought, 'What would that be like?'"

Luckily, The Doobie Brothers were under contract to Warner Brothers, a company that, in addition to producing music, also produced films.

Hearing about the band members' idea of dressing in old formal wear, Ted Templeman's production assistant, Venita Brazier, went to Warner Brothers' costume department. Armed with the sizes of each band member, she found the appropriate coats, shirts, hats — everything The Doobie Brothers needed for the photo shoot.

Not only did Brazier gather the clothes, but she also got a hold of the coach, the horses, and, along with the band's then-manager Bruce Cohn, scouted the perfect location for the photo session: Interstate 5 on the way out of Los Angeles, a stretch called "The Grapevine" on the southern end of the San Joaquin Valley.

A few years earlier, an earthquake had knocked down parts of the freeway, and Brazier had somehow secured permission from the proper authorities to use a not-yet-repaired section of the fallen freeway for *The Captain and Me* photo shoot.

"We thought it was a unique spot, so we got up next to the highest part of the freeway that was being rebuilt," said Simmons. "Handlers from Warner Brothers brought out the horses and the carriage. It was probably the most expensive album cover ever.

"We shot it in one day. It worked real well, though," said Simmons. "Tommy had written this song called 'The Captain and Me,' which was kind of a poetic, obtuse song. So we looked through the titles of the songs and we thought that it definitely worked in terms of this obscure reference to the captain. Who is the captain? I don't know. But it worked with the visual somehow and with how it all went down. It was kind of like these guys came in a time machine and landed on the freeway."

More than 40 years after the release of *The Captain and Me*, Simmons called it "a moment in time when we were hitting on all cylinders."

"There are a lot of great tracks on that record that we still enjoy playing live," he said. "At some point, songs from all our albums are incorporated as we go along into our shows now. But that record always seems to have certain songs that always turn up in the set, simply because they're more iconic or they're what people expect to hear.

"And we enjoy playing them because there's that moment of connection, to see the recognition on people's faces. That really means a lot to us as performers," said Simmons.

The 'Double Drum Song:' It's alive!

They Only Come Out at Night
The Edgar Winter Group

*T*t didn't have an official name, but Edgar Winter called it the "Double Drum Song." And even before it was recorded, it was played live at some pretty famous venues, like Woodstock and Royal Albert Hall.

A few years later, though, with his band The Edgar Winter Group, it would become Winter's biggest hit — under a different name.

In the late 1960s, Edgar was a member of his brother, Johnny's, band. It was then that he wrote what he called the "Double Drum Song."

"I wrote it as a sort of a walk-on with Johnny's band and I thought it was a cool riff," said Winter. "I played Hammond organ and alto sax and I did a dual drum solo with Johnny's drummer at the time, 'Uncle' John 'Red' Turner.

"So we used to call it the 'Double Drum Song' because of the dual drums. We played a version of it at Woodstock and we played it at Albert Hall [Royal Albert Hall in London]. And then we forgot about the thing for years."

Forgot about it, that is, until the advent of the synthesizer and its introduction into rock music in the 1970s. Winter was the first musician who had the idea to put a strap on a keyboard.

The Vinyl Dialogues

"It seems like such a simple and obvious idea that someone would have done it before. But no, it happened to be me. It was just one of those intuitive flashes," said Winter. "I was walking through the music store and I saw these new synthesizers, and one was in two pieces. It had a big control panel that was this really cool mad-scientist-looking contraption with all kinds of knobs and sliders and gauges. And then the keyboard was a separate piece.

"I picked it up and said, 'Wow, this doesn't weigh that much. It looks like you could put a strap on this and play it like a guitar,' which is exactly what I proceeded to do."

But Winter needed a song — a vehicle — for the synthesizer.

"And I thought, well, that old 'Double Drum Song,' I bet that would sound really good with that huge subsonic synth bottom."

So Winter started working up a live instrumental of the "Double Drum Song" to feature the synthesizer. The live version in the early days lasted anywhere from 15 to 20 minutes.

"I'll never forget the first night I walked onstage with that strap on the keyboard; the crowd just erupted," said Winter. "It was one of those real rock-and-roll moments. I said at that point, 'Oh, wow, we're really onto something here.'"

The song, according to Winter, was used basically as an exploration of the synthesizer. At the time, the synthesizer was controversial in the sense that some thought that the new electronic sound was dehumanizing the music, Winter said.

But he took a whole different approach.

"I said, 'Well, here's a new instrument; let's focus on trying to create new, unique sounds that have never been heard before in music.'"

124

So the "Double Drum Song" evolved. Every time Winter came up with a new sound, it dictated a section of the song. And he had names for the different sounds he was creating on the synthesizer - sounds that he called, for example, "acid bath" and the "kiss of death." Consequently, the song got longer and longer.

"Therefore, we thought that it wasn't something that was recordable or even that we'd want to record it," said Winter. "Plus, it had nothing to do with what we, The Edgar Winter Group, were all about."

But things changed when The Edgar Winter Group was recording its third studio album, *They Only Come Out at Night* in 1973.

By then the band included Johnny Badanjek and Chuck Ruff on drums; Rick Derringer on bass and pedal steel; Dan Hartman on guitar, bass and percussion; Randy Jo Hobbs on bass; and Ronnie Montrose on guitar and mandolin.

By the end of the project, Winter and Derringer — who produced the album — were talking about one more song to include.

"Rick suggested trying to come up with a version of the 'Double Drum Song' to put on the album because it was just killer," said Winter. "It was so powerful that we had to close the show with it every night. And Rick said, 'If it's in your show, it should be on the album.' And he was right. It was a crazy idea, but I love crazy ideas."

In the early 1970s, a lot of bands would go into the studio with two or three solid songs as a base and create the rest of the album in the studio, according to Winter. The cardinal rule then was that tape was always rolling because a band member would come up with something, and another band member would add a riff or another idea for a bridge, and on and on.

"So we happened to have two or three of those 15- to 20-minute versions of the thing — we were just calling

it 'the instrumental' by then — lying around," said Winter.
"It was a good excuse to get a little more blasted than
usual and have a big end-of-the-project editing party."

The technology that existed in that era was
limiting. The only way to edit something was to
physically cut the master tape, which, according to
Winter, was something like a surgical procedure. It
actually had to be cut with a razor blade and then spliced
back together with splicing tape. If somebody messed up
a part of the tape, it was gone forever.

"So we had the tapes in pieces lying all over the
control room, draped over the backs of chairs, over the
recording console and over the couch," said Winter. "We
were singing that old 'The foot bone connected to the
thigh bone' spiritual song when drummer Chuck Ruff
mumbled the immortal words: 'Wow, man, it's like
Frankenstein.'"

"There's the title of your song right there," said
Derringer to Winter.

"At first, I didn't like the idea," said Winter. "I
didn't like the connotation of the song being associated
with a monster, but then when I thought about it, I
thought, 'I'm the mad scientist doctor' and the song itself
is the monster creation. It just seemed to all make sense.

"As soon as Chuck said it, we played back the
song, and it was the perfect visual picture of Frankenstein.
You could just hear it. So the monster was born," said
Winter.

The "Double Drum Song," which devolved to
simply "the instrumental," had become "Frankenstein,"
which served as the final song on side two of *They Only
Come Out at Night*.

The album version was cut to 4:44, with the
released single version cut even further to just 3:28. The
song topped the charts at No. 1 in May 1973, and was The
Edgar Winter Group's only No. 1 single. The album *They*

Only Come Out at Night peaked at No. 3 on the U.S. T(
200 albums chart, the band's highest charting album.

The other single from the album, "Free Ride,"
written by Hartman, peaked at No. 14 on the pop singles
chart. But that was the song the band thought would be
the hit when it released the album.

"The thing is, after we completed the album, we
released 'Free Ride' thinking it would be the hit, and it
didn't go anywhere," said Winter. "Then we released two
or three subsequent singles that didn't do anything either.

"Finally, we released 'Frankenstein' on the B side
of 'Hangin' Around' [written by Winter and Hartman, the
first track on side one of the album] and 'Frankenstein'
started getting underground FM radio airplay. And the big
stations caught onto it. It was just this whole grassroots
movement that materialized out of nowhere."

"Frankenstein" was a song that just broke all the
rules, according to Winter.

"It's an instrumental to begin with and it's unique
in its own way," he said. "It's almost a precursor to heavy
metal, but with elements of jazz and classical. It almost
has what you would call 'movements' to it."

Winter added that the only reason "Frankenstein"
ever came into existence was because it was fun.

"It was something we loved to play and had it not
been for 'Frankenstein,' then 'Free Ride' would never
have been a hit," said Winter. "After 'Frankenstein' went
all the way to No. 1, we re-released 'Free Ride' and then
it, too, became a huge hit."

The iconic album cover of *They Only Come Out at
Night* features a shirtless and heavily made-up Winter,
with flowing blonde locks and bushy blonde sideburns
that would have made Elvis proud.

According to Winter, the cover was the concept of
famed fashion photographer Francesco Scavullo, who

devised similar album cover concepts for David Bowie and Alice Cooper records.

"I thought we were just going to do a photo session and take normal pictures," said Winter. "But at the end of the session, Francesco said, 'Let me try something different.'

"It was completely unplanned. At first, I said, 'You want to do *what*?' I thought it was crazy. Then I thought, 'It can't hurt to take the pictures.'

"But after I saw the picture, I was totally for it," said Winter. "I couldn't even believe it was me, it had such an unusual look. It really does have an impact. To me, it was a joke, a satirical comment on the times and one that I thought was kind of clever and cool. It was part of the whole Edgar Winter Group experience and it's perfect for the album title of *They Only Come Out at Night*."

To this day, Winter said, "Frankenstein" is still his favorite song.

"I think it's because only about five percent of it remains the same," he said. "It really is the perfect platform from which to explore and experiment. It's constantly evolving and constantly changing.

"It's become one of my trademarks. It has the long, never-ending scream and the guitar/vocal duo at the end of it."

The song and the band have been around for more than 40 years, and Winter doesn't see himself stopping anytime soon.

"The music doesn't get old to me," he said. "I love it every bit as much as I did when I first started out. I've always loved music just in and of itself. I love the beauty of the harmony in music.

"I think another thing that helps keep it fresh is the fact that what I've tried to do throughout my musical career is to play a wide variety of music and all styles of music.

"You'll never hear Edgar Winter talking about a farewell tour," he said. "I'm in it until the end. I come from the old bluesman mentality that when I'm 80 or 90, I'm going to be out there. It doesn't matter to me if it's a club on the corner or Madison Square Garden. If it's music, I'm there."

Creating havoc with the title's meaning

The Smoker You Drink, the Player You Get
Joe Walsh and Barnstorm

People have been asking Joe Vitale the same question for more than 40 years: What does the album title, *The Smoker You Drink, the Player You Get,* mean?

Well, blame that mass confusion on Joe Walsh.

"I think Joe did that on purpose because he kinda laughed about album titles that had all this deep meaning and all that, so he thought he would just pick a title that would create havoc with meaning. You know, 'What does this mean?' And it doesn't mean anything. It was just one of those Joe Walsh funny things," said Vitale.

The album, released in 1973, actually was by Walsh's band Barnstorm, but was credited on the album cover as a Joe Walsh solo project.

Walsh had left his first band, James Gang, in late 1971 to form Barnstorm with Vitale on drums, flute, and keyboards, and Kenny Passarelli on bass. Walsh and Vitale had known each other since the 1960s, when both were students at Kent State University.

Barnstorm's self-titled debut album, recorded at Caribou Ranch in Colorado, was released in 1972.

"Joe finished up with James Gang and wanted to do something solo and put a new band together. James Gang was a great band and they had a good run and I

131

think he just wanted to do something different. You
know, a lot of guys do that," said Vitale.

"I had known Joe for years before I worked with
him because we both were at Kent State University. We
grew up musically there. He was with James Gang and I
was doing other things. I went off to play with Ted
Nugent and the Amboy Dukes. All of a sudden, my time
freed up and he wanted to do something different, so we
formed Joe Walsh and Barnstorm and made the first
Barnstorm album.

"It was a great time back then in Colorado. There
was quite a music scene in the Denver-Boulder area.
There was all kinds of musicians who lived there. For
some reason, everybody moved to the mountains in the
early '70s," said Vitale.

The Smoker You Drink, the Player You Get was
Barnstorm's second album, and it featured what Vitale
called a "flagship song" in "Rocky Mountain Way."
Although the band was a trio for its first album,
Barnstorm added Rocke Grace on keyboards and vocals
for its second album.

According to Vitale, Walsh's favorite slide guitar
player at the time was Duane Allman of The Allman
Brothers Band. But Duane died in October 1971 in a
motorcycle accident at the age of 24 when his bike hit a
peach truck.

Allman's death had a huge impact on Walsh,
Vitale said.

"Joe figured we didn't have Duane anymore, so he
was going to have to pick up the slide guitar," said Vitale.
"Joe had never really played slide guitar up to then. He
started working on it, and at first he was struggling with
the tuning and all the stuff you have with a slide. But he's
a great guitar player, so he picked it up pretty quick."

When Barnstorm's producer, Bill Szymczyk, who
had also produced three James Gang albums, heard Walsh

on the slide guitar, he liked it — a lot. And he suggested
to the band members that they write a song that would
showcase Walsh's newfound talent on the slide guitar.

The song was "Rocky Mountain Way," which
peaked at No. 23 on the Billboard singles chart in 1973
and anchored the album *The Smoker You Drink, the
Player You Get*, which peaked at No. 6 on the Billboard
Hot 200 chart.

"We figured the best thing to write for slide guitar
at the time would have been a nice slow shuffle blues
thing," said Vitale. "We really didn't mean to write it as a
hit single. Who knows what's gonna happen with these
songs. We just wrote it as it was and Joe played really
well on it with the slide. It was the first recording that Joe
had ever played the slide on. Go figure — it turns out to be
his biggest song."

And Barnstorm loved that song.

"We loved the feel of it, we loved the sound of it,"
said Vitale. "Some songs are recorded and sometimes it
isn't necessarily the best song on the record or the best
song in general. But there is something about it that you
love. You like listening to it. 'Rocky Mountain Way'
sonically had this great vibe and an incredible feel.

"But we had no idea, we just figured, 'Wow, that's
a cool song,' and that people would like it because of the
same reasons we liked [it], and that was because we liked
listening to it because it sounded cool."

In addition to "Rocky Mountain Way," Vitale is
credited with writing two other songs on *The Smoker You
Drink, the Player You Get*: "Book Ends" and "Days Gone
By." And he doesn't hesitate giving Walsh credit for those
songs as well.

"Those were fun songs to work on. Me and Joe
both wrote those. He liked what I was doing and I liked
what he was doing," said Vitale. "We figured we were a
band now; let's try to merge some of this material. That's

basically all it is. He needed songs for the record and there were a couple of spots open for some songs. I had a bunch of material and he listened to my material and he liked those two songs so we did them."

The Smoker You Drink, the Player You Get has a mixture of several styles of music, including blues, jazz, folk, pop, and Caribbean music. And that was by design, Vitale said.

"Our producer [Szymczyk] used to call it the 40-minute radio show. It's like 40 minutes of odds and ends, different styles and all that," said Vitale.

"But I don't know if that works anymore because of the way people make records now, especially the younger people. They've got a [singular] vibe and a style, and I guess their fans don't want to hear anything else."

Vitale cites a group like Nine Inch Nails, which he says has a singular vibe and style that the band is really fantastic at conveying, and the band members stick with it.

"You know, with a Beatles record — and all kinds of records made back then — there was this variety show on the record. I kind of liked that because it showed the different sides of the musicians and different styles. You could tell it was the same group, but it ventured off into different things. I think that's kind of over now. I think groups now kind of stick to their styles," said Vitale.

"A good example would have been someone like The Police. They had a sound and a style and they really never ventured too far from that. And they did it so well, and people loved it," he said. "But in the '60s and '70s, people were really, really creative and trying all kinds of things."

Barnstorm would record only one more album after *The Smoker You Drink, the Player You Get*, although the lines were always somewhat blurred between what was a Barnstorm album and what was a Joe Walsh solo album.

"What happened was that management and the record company wanted to gear it more toward Joe as a solo, which kind of changed the format of the band. We kind of departed for a while. Kenny went off to [do] other things and so did Rocke. And I continued working with Joe," said Vitale. "We made a whole bunch of solo records after that, including *So What, There Goes the Neighborhood* and *Ordinary Average Guy*. I made tons of records with him.

"But as far as Barnstorm — we made the first album, then we made the second album as Joe Walsh, but it was still us guys. Then *So What* was the same thing — as Joe Walsh.

"I think it was just for business. The management and record companies wanted to keep Joe as a solo. It didn't matter to me; we were still working together," said Vitale.

After Barnstorm, Vitale followed Walsh to The Eagles and played drums and keyboards in the group's road band, and co-wrote with Walsh the song "Pretty Maids All in a Row" that appeared on The Eagles' 1976 *Hotel California* album. Vitale also played on the 1977 Crosby, Stills and Nash album *CSN,* and later worked with Peter Frampton and Dan Fogelberg, among others.

But more than 40 years later, *The Smoker You Drink, the Player You Get* still rocks with the best albums of the era, Vitale said.

"I think it stands up, I think it holds as much weight today as it did then," said Vitale. "It's a good record to listen to. When you hear that stuff on the radio now, it sounds fantastic. It's amazing, with all the technology that we didn't have back then, to hear that today, it holds up. Anything from the *Smoker* album on the radio today — and they play a lot of it on the radio — it sounds fantastic.

"It meets all the standards of today. That's one of my favorite records that I ever made," he said.

Uniting the stoner crowd and the hoops crowd

Los Cochinos
Cheech & Chong

*J*ack Nicholson's reckless driving was the inspiration for a hit single on a Grammy Award-winning comedy album that featured one of the Beatles on lead guitar.

The album, *Los Cochinos*, released in 1973 by the iconic comedy team Cheech & Chong, featured the single "Basketball Jones," with a lead guitar intro by George Harrison.

Like Hollywood A-lister Nicholson, Cheech & Chong were big fans of the 1972-73 Los Angeles Lakers. The team that season featured future National Basketball Association Hall of Famers Wilt Chamberlain and Jerry West, and finished first in the Pacific Division with a 60-22 record.

Cheech & Chong were in Nicholson's car one evening on the way to The Forum, where the Lakers played their home games. They were running late and in jeopardy of missing the opening tipoff.

"Cheech was in the back seat and I was on the passenger side front," said Chong. "And Cheech got nervous because Jack started driving on the wrong side of the road because we were late for the game. There was a big lineup to get into the [Forum] parking lot and so Jack pulled out into the oncoming traffic. He drove a good mile into oncoming traffic."

At the time, there was an R&B/soul group called Brighter Side of Darkness, a band mostly made up of high school students that formed in Chicago. In 1972, the group released a single called "Love Jones," which reached No. 3 on the Hot Soul Singles chart and was certified gold in early 1973.

"We had been in Jack Nicholson's car before and he drives like a maniac," said Cheech. "There was this song called 'Love Jones' at the time and I was always singing different tunes and parodies and trying to do different voices.

"Jack was driving on the wrong side of the street and up on the sidewalk. And I started singing, 'Basketball Jones, I got a Basketball Jones,'" said Cheech.

"And I was in the front seat and I was kind of horrified at Jack's driving and laughing at Cheech's 'Basketball Jones' song in the background," said Chong. "Cheech said, 'That's funny; we got to record that.' So I wrote the rest of the lyrics and I think the next day we went in and recorded it."

Los Cochinos was Cheech & Chong's third comedy album, following their self-titled debut album in 1971 and *Big Bambu* in 1972.

Los Cochinos was recorded at A&M Records on North La Brea Avenue near Sunset Boulevard in Hollywood. The album was produced by Lou Adler, who managed the careers of Cheech & Chong as well as Sam Cooke, Carole King, and The Mamas and the Papas, among others.

So Adler knew a lot of artists, and he knew a lot of artists who were in the A&M studio recording at the same time Cheech & Chong was cutting *Los Cochinos*.

When it came time to record "Basketball Jones," Adler started calling in favors. He called Carole King and he called Michelle Phillips from The Mamas and the Papas. And he went through the studio rounding up the

138

likes of Billy Preston, Klaus Voormann, Jim Karstein, Jim
Keltner and . . . George Harrison.

"He called everybody. And he got George," said
Chong. "And Lou said, 'George, we need an introduction
to the song.' And George listened to the record, and he sat
down and played that great intro. And then someone
asked him, 'What do you think of Cheech & Chong?' And
he said, 'I suppose they're funny.' He didn't get the joke.
But he played a beautiful intro.

"It was a big coming together," said Chong. "It was
a product of the times. That's what was happening then."

Chong and Harrison had met before. In fact,
Chong had met all The Beatles by 1973.

"I must have smoked with George a good half-
dozen times, maybe more, where we sat around and
shared a joint, shared the moment," said Chong. "I knew
him more than the rest of The Beatles. I've met Ringo and
I met John briefly at a party, but I really only hung with
George. The only Beatle I never got high with was Paul,
and that's on my bucket list."

It wasn't an accident that Cheech & Chong's
comedy albums often featured musical bits, because both
were musically trained. "Basketball Jones" wasn't a
stretch for them at all.

In fact, Cheech & Chong had released comedy
singles before, starting in 1971 with "Santa Claus and His
Old Lady," which was only released as a single and was
not included on the duo's debut eponymous album that
same year. The B-side of the single was "Dave," which
would become one of Cheech & Chong's most famous
bits, and which was included on the debut album.

"We put it ['Santa Claus and His Old Lady'] out
and it caused a big sensation, but it was mainly on FM
radio because FM then was underground and played all
this underground stuff," said Cheech. "What was cool was
that we started getting AM Top 40 play with 'Basketball

Jones.' And we started being expected to have hit singles. We were a comedy group and we were making hit Top 40 singles. 'Basketball Jones' went pretty high [No. 15 on the Hot 100] on the charts. People loved it and it was played in a lot of basketball stadiums. It just kind of endured."

Instead of creating pressure on Cheech & Chong to produce more hit singles in addition to hit albums, the two of them welcomed the challenge.

"It wasn't pressure [to make more hit singles], it was opportunity," said Cheech. "All of sudden, we thought, OK, this is possible. It was possible for us to have comedy hit singles. How cool? So let's keep doing it."

No other comedy acts at the time were producing hit singles.

"Most of the comedians, our contemporaries, would record their live act," said Cheech. "Lily Tomlin, George Carlin, Richard Pryor, Steve Martin — they would record their live act. But we went into the studio with different scenarios and it was totally different. So it was easy for us to go, OK, let's put some music and some arrangements together and go for it. It didn't fit the comedy format. Ours was music."

Cheech thinks that makes a pretty solid case for Cheech & Chong being in the Rock and Roll Hall of Fame.

"But people say, 'They're not musical.' What the fuck do you mean we're not musical? We have four hit singles and other bands cover our stuff."

Los Cochinos, featuring "Basketball Jones," won a Grammy for Best Comedy Recording in 1974, at the 16th annual Grammy Awards ceremony.

"I think 'Basketball Jones' really put us on the map," said Chong. "It appealed to the sports crowd. We'd always appealed to the stoner crowd. But that was the first time that there was a record where those cultures came

together. All those NBA basketball players were big
pothead, fun-loving guys. And they still are.

"With 'Basketball Jones,' it was perfect, man.
They all loved it. We talked about Chickie Hearn and all
those guys in the record. Falling into the popcorn
machine. It was a good time."

That period of Cheech & Chong's history holds
fond memories for both artists.

"It was so much fun. It was almost kind of like a
blur. We were touring constantly, always on the road, and
we were recording," said Cheech. "We'd record on the
road. It was like, OK, it's time for another album.
Whenever we came home, we'd go into the studio and
record as much as we could. We'd go out on tour and find
an album studio on the road someplace. We'd bring the
microphones into our hotel rooms and record. I have a
hard time sometimes remembering what went on which
album. We were touring up to 300 days a year and
recording on the road and it was a blur.

"I remember Adler said — we were on this pace
putting out an album a year — and he said, 'If you guys
have one weakness, it's that you don't record enough.'
When do you want us to record more?" said Cheech.

Chong appreciates the history surrounding his
career, and tries to stay humble about the iconic evolution
of Cheech & Chong.

"What you have to do, you have to appreciate the
fact that people know you, love you, and want to take
your picture. And if that bothers you in any way, then it's
difficult. But I don't mind at all. I learned that being
humble is the best approach to anything," said Chong.

"And just to be thankful that people do recognize
you and do want your picture. Because there are millions
of people on this planet that would love to be in your
position. To me, every day is a joy because I've been on
the other side of it and I know what it's like to be turned

down by some famous guy. All you want to do is tell him how much you love him. And it's like you've intruded into his space, you know. So I know that feeling. And I will never, ever put that on anybody. I don't care what I'm doing, even if I'm late for a plane, I'll stop for a picture."

Joining the legendary comedy duo on stage for the October 2013 show at the Keswick Theatre in Glenside, PA, was Tommy Chong's wife, comedian Shelby Chong.
(Photo by Mike Morsch)

Cheech & Chong hang out with the author after their October 2013 show at the Keswick Theatre in Glenside, PA.
(Photo by Kevin Hughes)

Finally getting to the 'egg-and-bacon take'

Holiday
America

There were days during long recording sessions when Dewey Bunnell would look forward to the "egg-and-bacon take."

Bunnell, Gerry Beckley, and Dan Peek — the band America — were recording their fourth studio album, *Holiday,* in 1974 at AIR Studios in London. They were working with legendary record producer George Martin, who had produced all of The Beatles' original albums.

Bunnell remembers it as a special time. During the days of recording the album, he and his bandmates would frequent a little cafe in the area or eat at the studio commissary.

And they'd frequently eat bacon and eggs.

"We say 'bacon and eggs,' but the British say 'egg and bacon.' Every day we'd do some takes and George would say, 'Right lads, one more take.' And we'd say, 'But George, we're getting hungry.' And he'd say, 'OK, this is the egg-and-bacon take.'"

The band's eponymous 1971 debut album had been produced by Ian Samwell, a British songwriter and guitarist who had worked with Sir Cliff Richard; after relocating to Los Angeles, their second and third albums, *Homecoming* in 1972 and *Hat Trick* in 1973, were produced by the band members themselves.

"Gerry and Dan and I produced the second and third albums and we realized we were spending a lot of money," said Bunnell. "Producing records isn't just about saying, 'Oh, that sounds good, let's put a tambourine on the next track.' There's a lot of administrative work and booking studio time and paying bills and all that kind of stuff.

"By the time we got to the third album, we said, 'This is too much work. We need a producer,'" said Bunnell.

America was going to start at the top in its search for a producer and was hoping to get George Martin to sign on.

And timing is everything.

David Geffen — who had managed Crosby, Stills and Nash as well as Laura Nyro — was also America's manager at the time.

Geffen knew Martin well enough to arrange for him to meet Beckley, Bunnell, and Peek. Incidentally, Geffen would go on to create Asylum Records in 1970, Geffen Records in 1980, DGC Records in 1990, and become one of the three founders — along with Steven Spielberg and Jeffrey Katzenberg — of DreamWorks SKG Studios in 1994.

"We were these young whippersnappers and George was coming out of the Beatles thing — it had been a few years since they had broken up — and he was basically available," said Bunnell.

And after working with The Beatles, Martin finished a project with a band called Seatrain, and was looking around for his next project as well.

He was in Los Angeles for the 46th Academy Awards show when Geffen approached him to meet America's principals. Martin had scored the soundtrack to the James Bond film *Live and Let Die,* the title track of which was written by Paul and Linda McCartney. The song was nominated for "Best Original Song" that year, but lost the Oscar to "The Way We Were" by Marvin Hamlisch.

Martin met with the band and, according to Bunnell, formed an instant rapport. Bunnell said he thought that it may have been because of a common bond: he, Beckley, and Peek were all children of American servicemen who had British wives, and they had first met and formed the band while all their fathers were stationed at the United States Air Force Base at RAF West Ruislip, London.

"So we hit it off and he said, 'Sure, but I understand you spent a lot of time on your last album. I must ask that you come to London and we record it in my studio.'"

Once they reached an agreement, Bunnell said that the band members wanted to make sure they were ready to record by the time they got to London. They hunkered down and honed and arranged their material, and by the time they got to London, they were ready to go.

"We had arranged the songs the way we liked to do things, with the vocal harmonies and the acoustic guitar stuff," said Bunnell. "And George took it from there. He was very impressed that we were prepared. I think we did the whole album in less than three weeks — 17 days or something like that. Mixed and ready to go. And George said, 'Well, this is nice.'"

Bunnell called the *Holiday* recording sessions lighthearted but structured.

"When we were making the third album [*Hat Trick*] in Los Angeles at the Record Plant, it was party time," said Bunnell. "Late sessions. And the Record Plant was a cool place to hang out.

"But the British studio — AIR Studios in London — it was like we were in some kind of factory," he said. "It was very sterile and weird. George was from that school having produced The Beatles, and he still had a lot of that work ethic going on, which was good because it reined us in."

Besides the fact that the band was in awe of Martin, Bunnell said that Martin was from a different generation.

"He was this princely guy," said Bunnell. "Sweet and nice and full of anecdotes. We realized right away that it was all business here. We like to say that he sophisticated the sound, if you will, because with George you got an arranger in terms of symphony and orchestral arrangements."

One of Martin's favorite phrases, Bunnell said, was "Don't gild the lily." Martin wasn't one of those guys who wanted to keep layering stuff on a song. "If you've got a nice tasty thing, an overdub or a vocal that works, let's not bury it under a lot of varnish," Bunnell recalled Martin saying.

The album hit big in the United States and reached No. 3 on the Billboard album chart. It produced two hit singles, the Bunnell-penned "Tin Man," which reached No. 4 on the Billboard singles chart and No. 1 on the adult contemporary chart; and "Lonely People," written by Peek and his wife, Catherine, which charted at No. 5 on the Billboard singles chart and No. 1 on the adult contemporary chart.

"Tin Man" was based on the general theme of *The Wizard of Oz*, which Bunnell said has always been, and is still today, one of his favorite movies.

"I love that film and the whole premise of people having those things already in them that they seem to be desperately seeking — courage and love and all those things," said Bunnell.

Bunnell likes his songs to paint pictures — and he likes a lyric that takes the listener some place in his own mind within the first few lines of a song.

And then there's the great grammar in "Tin Man."

"I always say I don't know where my grammar really comes from, other than maybe in and of itself, it's colorful. 'Oz never did give nothing to the Tin Man, that he didn't, didn't already have,'" said Bunnell. "It's sort of poetic license because I really don't speak that way."

Bunnell thought "Tin Man" had a catchy melody and was a strong enough song — with its chord progression — going into the recording session.

"I'm not a schooled musician, so I'm not using music theory and things. I'm really not applying certain musical-mathematical equations when I write a song," he said. "A little more now because I'm self-training even more. But then, though, it was finding some chords that sounded good together. It was all just throwing the dart at the board and saying, 'Oh, I think I got a bullseye there.'"

Creative album covers were still the norm in the 1970s, and when it came time to decide what the *Holiday* cover would look like, the band members agreed that specific lyrics from the Beckley-written song "What Does It Matter" would be an appropriate concept for the cover: "Look, the lady's got a photograph, silver-framed, velvet-backed."

"So we all agreed — hey, let's make sure the cover kind of mirrors that lyrical imagery: silver-framed, velvet-backed," said Bunnell. "So now we have to stick a photograph in that frame. Of course, in those days, they always wanted the artists to be on the album cover. Now, the last thing we want is our picture on the album because we're older."

Because the songs — especially with Martin's arrangements — had an old-time feel, Bunnell, Beckley, and Peek decided to wear clothes that reflected a time gone by. They secured an old car from a collector who rented cars for just that purpose — publicity shoots — and headed out to Hyde Park in London.

149

"The costumes showed up, the car showed up, and we shot the cover," said Bunnell.

But Bunnell, Beckley, and Peek aren't the only ones pictured on the cover. A closer look reveals a fourth person, barely visible, sitting in the car. It's the band's drummer, Willie Leacox.

"Management and agents are always wanting to condense the artists into who they are," said Bunnell. "They don't want to muddy the waters and have the public think that Willie is a permanent member of the band. Gerry, Dan, and I started the band and we were the writers and we were the ones signed and our names are on the contracts. But as friends and buddies, we really wanted Willie to be with us. We still wanted to be the principals, but we wanted everybody to know that he was in the band, too. And he's still with us."

It was indeed a special and heady time for the members of America.

"Right now, as we reach this age, it's just fun to realize that so many things did happen, and how they are still viable parts of this giant puzzle that is the pop music business," said Bunnell.

"Going into the AIR Studios equipment room and picking out something, like we needed a bell for a song — and, by the way, that's the bell we used on 'Yellow Submarine;' wow, cool, we're using the 'Yellow Submarine' bell — George made all that very fun."

Bunnell said that every generation thinks its music scene was better than any other generation.

"The fact that the songs are still viable and inspiring to other artists, I don't know when that will end," he said. "I think the personalities do somewhat go away — except for the super superstars. But I think the music will always have a place."

150

The high energy and up-tempo of early disco

Self-titled
KC and the Sunshine Band

If you lived in the southeastern United States in the late 1960s and were buying records, there's a pretty good chance that Harry Wayne Casey boxed up those vinyl records and shipped them to your local record store, where you purchased them.

Casey was working at TK Records in Miami, a wholesale record company that supplied everything vinyl to the southeastern part of the country through Tone Distributors, a huge independent wholesale record distributor.

"Whenever you bought a record, it probably came from our warehouse," said Casey. "It came from the pressing plant to us, and we made sure all the record stores in the southeast got their records.

"So there's probably a possibility that I pulled that record and put it in the order that you eventually bought," he said.

And that starting-in-the-mailroom experience turned out to be the foundation of the musical education for Harry Wayne Casey that would directly lead to the formation of KC and the Sunshine Band in 1973. That was when KC began writing songs with Richard Finch, a bassist who was also an engineer at TK Records. Guitarist Jerome Smith and drummer Robert Johnson, both studio musicians at TK Records, joined to create the Sunshine Band.

The first Casey-Finch collaboration, "Blow Your Whistle," went to No. 15 on the R&B charts. Another single, "Blow Your Funky Horn" was released in February 1974, and experienced so much success that the band planned to cut an album.

"I was consumed by music, period. Not so much playing, but listening to records and wanting to be around every facet of music," said Casey. "What got all-consuming was that I wrote a big hit for George McCrae."

That hit, "Rock Your Baby," released in May 1974, reached No. 1 on the Billboard Hot 100 singles chart by July 1974, where it stayed for two weeks.

"So now I was doing songs for KC and the Sunshine Band and George McCrae, and then other artists wanted us to do stuff for them and I became even more consumed in all of it," said Casey.

During that time, Casey said it was somewhat rare for an artist to write all the music and produce it as well. Most artists who had achieved that level of fame, he said, had other people writing and producing albums for them.

"They would have a few cuts on an album that they wrote, but I don't know how many of them were writing all their own stuff and producing it themselves," said Casey.

"I had been around for years prior to that, so it all felt very natural to me," he said. "I had studied this, I lived it. So by the time I was ready to do it for myself, it just seemed like the natural thing to do. It was almost like I had a complete understanding of how it's done and how to do it.

"I was at a recording studio hanging out and I got to see things first-hand — how things were done. And I definitely picked up on all of that."

KC and the Sunshine Band's first album, *Do It Good*, released in 1974, didn't make much of an impact in mainstream America, but the song "Queen of Clubs" off that album did well enough that the album was reissued under the name *Queen of Clubs* — with a different album cover.

In 1975 the band released its second studio album, the self-titled *KC and the Sunshine Band,* which featured the mega-hits "That's The Way (I Like It)," "Get Down Tonight," and "Boogie Shoes."

While cutting tracks for the eponymous *KC and the Sunshine Band,* Casey was continuing to live and breathe music.

"We had some minor success with the first album, especially in Europe, so this was just the obligation to do the next album for the record company," said Casey.

Casey said if one listens to *Do It Good* and then to *KC and the Sunshine Band,* one can hear a distinct difference between the albums.

"Something drastically changed, both vocally and creatively, for me," he said. "I don't know if I went about the second album in a different way or if it just flowed differently.

I don't know if it was growth or that I finally found myself. I wasn't screaming on the first album, but I sang a lot harder and with a lot more force. On the second album, I sang with not as much force."

The whole idea behind the *KC and the Sunshine Band* album was to include only high-energy, up-tempo songs.

"I set out to bring some energy to the music," said Casey. "I felt music had gotten really dark and I just wanted to bring some life back into the music. That was my goal, to do that, and I think that's what we did. It [the album] opened a lot of doors and a lot of eyes. A lot of people said, 'Yeah, I like that,' and they started emulating it and creating this high-energy type of sound."

It was the early stages of what we now know as disco music. And initially, "Get Down Tonight" entered the Billboard chart at only No. 98 and went off the chart the following week.

Casey was concerned.

"I went to the head of the record company and said, 'But this is a smash record,'" said Casey. "And he said, 'Don't worry about it.' And that was it."

The song, originally titled "What You Want Is What You Get," was changed to "Get Down Tonight," re-entered the charts in short order, and became the first of five No. 1 hits that KC and the Sunshine Band would have. The second album captured that high-energy characteristic that Casey was hoping to achieve.

The fact that Casey had been writing songs, doing session work and had already had success on the charts with McCrae's "Rock Your Baby," helped prepare Casey for his own No. 1 single. The album *KC and the Sunshine Band* itself made it to No. 4 on the charts in the U.S.

"I had witnessed what happens when a record goes to No. 1, the excitement of it where you sell a million copies," said Casey. "I think it helped me a lot in my growth and my understanding of the record business, being around all this stuff. One minute you have a hit record, the next minute it's not, and then you can have another hit record."

The album cover for *KC and the Sunshine Band* was fairly basic. Casey said he had some input, but the graphic designer who designed the band's logo had been hired to create the cover. The cover featured just the band's name and some splashes of rainbow colors that weren't particularly over the top, like some of the color schemes of the mid-1970s.

The funky mid-'70s costumes that became part of the whole KC and the Sunshine Band package, however, were a different story. The costumes had what Casey described as "pizzazz."

"If you saw our first *Midnight Special* appearance, we wore street clothes. Myself, I wore jeans and a T-shirt all the time," said Casey.

But when they started to experience some success, Casey hired clothing designer Harvey-Louis Krantz, who was designing costumes for a lot of the country music stars of the era.

"One thing you do when you're a group and you make it big is that you hire people to do your clothing," said Casey. "Harvey was the one who really brought all that pizzazz and everything to our outfits. Somebody said he would be a perfect fit for us, and with our input and his great designs came our outfits.

"He made sure everybody had a different color on, but that it all coordinated with me. If you look at his stuff today, it's still the same stuff we wore 40 years ago."

Once Krantz had made his contribution to the KC and the Sunshine Band look, Casey then worked with designer Fleur Thiemeyer on his clothes. She had designed clothes for Olivia Newton-John and Rod Stewart.

"You find these people to put you together. It's all kind of part of the process. Some people just wear jeans or whatever comes out of their closet. I just wanted something a little bit more than that."

A single from the *KC and the Sunshine Band* album became a disco standard three years after its release.

"Boogie Shoes," written and produced by Casey and Finch, became a hit when it was included in the soundtrack of the 1977 film *Saturday Night Fever*, starring John Travolta. The song was released as a single in January 1978 and was a Billboard Top 40 hit for the band.

According to Casey, it could have just as easily been KC and the Sunshine Band's 1976 single, "Shake Your Booty" — which would be the band's third No. 1 single — that appeared in *Saturday Night Fever*.

"They [the producers of *Saturday Night Fever*] wanted to put 'Shake Your Booty' on the soundtrack album," said Casey. "At the time, it was getting ready to come out as a single. So we said, 'How about "Boogie Shoes?"' and they went with it. It was just pretty much a phone call."

In 2012, "Boogie Shoes," along with the entire soundtrack of *Saturday Night Fever*, was inducted into the National Recording Registry of the United States Library of Congress. The selections for the 2012 registry brought the total number of recordings there to 375. The selections represent a diverse array of spoken-word and musical recordings, from nearly every musical category during the years 1918 through 1980.

In the nearly 40 years since the release of *KC and the Sunshine Band*, Casey said the band still doesn't get the credit it deserves for being an integral part of the creation of the disco genre.

"We still don't get a lot of recognition for a lot of the things that we did and were a part of," said Casey. "A lot of times, it's given to the Bee Gees or whoever. KC and the Sunshine Band kind of gets left in the dark."

Sometimes, Casey said, he feels like the Rodney Dangerfield of the music business.

"I do get a lot of respect, but in a lot of ways, we get no respect and no recognition and everybody just wants to cast us aside and give us no credibility for doing anything, from writing great songs or anything," he said.

Critics constantly tear him apart, he said, for his songs and his lyrics.

"My songs were no more simple than The Beatles' 'She Loves You, Yeah-Yeah-Yeah.' I just chose to write commercial-sounding songs," said Casey.

That desire, he admitted, actually came from his background working in retail. People used to come into the record distribution center where he worked in Miami in the early days and try to hum a song without having any idea of the name of the song.

"I wanted to make sure they knew what the name of the song was," he said. "That's why I wrote more commercial songs."

E.E. Lawson: Eggs, chicks, chicks, hens

It'll Shine When It Shines
Ozark Mountain Daredevils

T here was a time in his life in the early 1970s when Steve Cash lived with some other hippies in a ramshackle building about 40 miles east of Springfield, Missouri. The place used to be a general store in the 1920s, and stood on a lonely road out in the middle of nowhere.

While cleaning out the place to make it habitable, Cash found an old receipt book from its days as a general store. Printed on the receipt book were the words: "E.E. Lawson: Eggs, chicks, chicks, hens."

"It just stuck in my mind. I said to myself, 'There's something there. There's a song or a poem in there or something,'" said Cash.

A few years later, in 1974, Cash and the other members of The Ozark Mountain Daredevils – John Dillon, Larry Lee, Randle Chowning, Michael "Supe" Granda, and Buddy Brayfield – had converged on a place called Ruedi Valley Ranch, a pre-Civil War house outside of Aldrich, Missouri, to record the band's second album, *It'll Shine When It Shines*.

The band was coming off some moderate success with its self-titled debut album, *The Ozark Mountain Daredevils,* in 1973. The album featured the single, "If You Wanna Get to Heaven," which reached No. 25 on the Billboard singles chart that year. That first album was recorded in London and produced by Glyn Johns, who by that point in his career, had already worked with the likes of The Beatles, The Rolling Stones, The Who, and Bob Dylan.

When Johns asked The Ozark Mountain Daredevils where they wanted to record their second album, the band members had an idea.

"When we recorded the first album, we packed up the wives and girlfriends and took off for London and just had the time of our lives," said Cash. "Supe hadn't even been on an airplane before. We were over there for about a month to six weeks, or something like that, and it was just incredible.

"But when Glyn asked where we wanted to record the second album, we said, 'Well, we did the first one at your place, why don't we do the second one at our place?'"

The band had become accustomed to rehearsing at Ruedi Valley Ranch because band member Randle Chowning and his brother, Rusty, were living there. And that was where they chose to record that second album, *It'll Shine When It Shines*.

"Glyn said, 'Sure, that sounds like fun. Let's do that. I'll get some mobile trucks from L.A. and we'll just bring them right there and we'll set up at the house.' We didn't know what we were doing and he didn't either. He was just making it up as he went along."

So in the summer of 1974, the wives and girlfriends once again joined the band at Ruedi Valley Ranch, which was big enough to accommodate the band members and their significant others, and even an elderly woman named Lydia who helped out by cooking the meals for the group.

It took nearly two weeks to record the album, time enough that laundry needed to be done at least once during that period. Cash's wife was about seven months pregnant with the couple's first child and physical chores became difficult, so Cash volunteered to drive into Aldrich to do the laundry.

"We had this old Volkswagen, and on the way back into town that morning to do the laundry, those lines [from the old receipt book] came to me just out of the blue," said Cash. "I was just driving. And I started to write this song in my head."

By the time Cash got back to Ruedi Valley Ranch, he had a clean load of laundry in the Volkswagen and a complete song written in his head. Upon returning to the house, Cash, Chowning, and Dillon worked up an a cappella version of the song and then played it for Johns. At 2 p.m. they began to record the song, and the whole thing was done by 5 p.m. that same day.

The entire song, eventually titled "E.E. Lawson," and which included the words that Cash had seen in the old receipt book years earlier — "Eggs, chicks, chicks, hens" — took only 12 to 14 hours from inception to completion.

Other times, it was the simple things during the recording sessions that took center stage, like on the single, "It Couldn't Be Better," written by Dillon and Elizabeth Anderson.

"We recorded that song on the front porch," said Cash. "It was June, so all the bugs were out. But we wanted to record it like John wrote it, from his front porch. So we actually set up on the front porch of the ranch [house]."

Johns set up the microphones on the porch and even put a couple more microphones in the yard, just to pick up the sounds of the crickets.

"When you listen to that song, you can hear the crickets," said Cash. "Everybody thought we'd have to take those out when we were mixing, but when we got into the studio everybody agreed we should leave those cricket sounds in the song."

And it was that type of creativity, simplicity, and execution that was the standard for *It'll Shine When It Shines.*

"That was happening every single day," said Cash. "Even the single, 'It'll Shine When It Shines' that John [Dillon] and I wrote, was written in one morning. We wrote the first half of it in the morning, finished it up in the early afternoon, and then started recording it. That happened on song after song.

"So much was happening there all at once. We were inspiring each other without limits. Every day it was like, 'Listen to this! Listen to this!' It was incredible. It was like the faucet had been turned on."

It was within the context of this creative rush that the song "Jackie Blue" would emerge. Unbeknownst to the band members at the time, "Jackie Blue" would be the group's highest-charting single in its history, reaching No. 3 on the Billboard Hot 100 in 1975.

Drummer Larry Lee had written the original melody for "Jackie Blue" on the piano. But when he played it for Johns, the producer heard something different.

"Actually it was just another song that we had," said Cash. "We had so many to pick and choose from. But Glyn heard something that none of the rest of us heard. I think he heard 'pop song' in his brain because he said, 'We gotta do that one.'"

Lee had some of the song's lyrics written, and they were actually about a guy named "Jackie Blue," who was a drug dealer. But by the time the band left Ruedi Valley Ranch, the song wasn't completed. Band members traveled to Los Angeles to finish some lead guitar parts and everything was progressing on the song except for one thing: there were no lead vocals because Lee hadn't yet finished the lyrics.

Sitting at the control panel in the recording studio in Los Angeles, Johns asked Cash if Lee had finished "Jackie Blue."

"And I said no," said Cash. "So Glyn said, 'Get over there and [help Lee] finish that song.'"

Lee sat down at the piano and played Cash what he had completed so far of "Jackie Blue." Together they tried to finish the song.

"I said, first of all, we're going to change it," said Cash. "It's not gonna be about a guy, it's got to be a girl. Then we started over with some of the lyrics he already had, switched them around, and I wrote a couple of verses. We finally finished it, went back into the studio, and recorded it."

Cash said he realized that "Jackie Blue" was a "radio song," one that had a good chance to get wide airplay.

"It was completely different than a lot of the other music we played, both live and on records up to that point. But it had something; it had a hook to it."

Cash said the single took off on its own without the help of the album's label, A&M Records. A couple of disc jockeys in Chicago and Baltimore started playing the song in their on-air rotations.

"And it just took off on its own," said Cash. "It would have gotten to No. 1, I think, but Elton John kept us from getting to No. 1. I think he had 'Philadelphia Freedom' out at that time.

I think the song is well done, but it's not my personal favorite of all our songs, but that doesn't mean anything," said Cash.

"We always did a really diverse catalog of music. We had all these styles that everybody had from where they grew up."

163

Cash said that the band would have what he called "title parties" — usually at the end of the recording session — when it came time to name an album.

"Those parties were absurd and ridiculous," said Cash. "It would basically digress to 'What about Ralph the Rubber Neighbor?' Nobody could get serious about it."

But the single "It'll Shine When It Shines" sort of defined the whole experience of recording the album.

"It was written in one day and it was really written about the lifestyle and the life we believed in — and still do — that we were actually living at the time," said Cash. "The lyrics to that song are pretty much what we believed. It was from the heart, without a doubt. I still think it's one of our best songs. By the end of the recording session, it was pretty apparent that was the kind of song that encapsulated the whole spirit of the adventure."

The cover of the album features a picture of an older woman, arms out, kind of posing for the picture. That's Lydia, the woman who cooked meals for the band members while they were recording the album at Ruedi Valley Ranch.

"She lived just down the road from where the ranch was," said Cash. "Jim Mayfield, our photographer, kept hounding her because he was taking pictures all over the place. And she wouldn't let him take her picture until the last day of recording. She was just sitting out front relaxing and Jim kept hounding her until she finally said, 'You can take one.' So he took that picture.

"When we were looking at all the photographs for the cover, it was unanimous — that was the cover photo. It was just Lydia being Lydia," said Cash. "I think she really enjoyed the experience because she had recently lost her adult son that she had cared for. He had passed away and I think she really enjoyed the experience of being one of the girls."

Cash said he thinks *It'll Shine When It Shines*
defines The Ozark Mountain Daredevils as a group.

"We're still playing and people still come to hear
those songs," he said. "The diehard fans can't get enough
of those songs. I hate the word 'iconic' — it's overused —
but that album is sort of iconic in that sense. It defines an
era of hippie bands and people — as naive as it might
seem in hindsight — that really believed [in] those things
and that music."

The epitome of a 'slow ride' to New York

Fool for the City
Foghat

ang-bang-bang-bang. That was drummer Roger Earl's contribution to Foghat's highest-charting single, "Slow Ride," and he is proud of it.

Earl and bandmate Rod Price owned a house in Long Island, and had the basement soundproofed. It was there that the band — "Lonesome Dave" Peverette, Earl, Price, and Tony Stevens — was getting ready to record its fifth album, *Fool for the City*. But then Tony Stevens left the band because of its nonstop tour schedule, and he was replaced by Nick Jameson.

"We had the basement soundproofed and Nick had just joined the band," said Earl. "We were just jamming, like a John Lee Hooker riff. The whole arrangement for 'Slow Ride' that night was just the same that came out on the record. And then Dave said, 'I think I've got some words for that.' And that's how the song was born.

"Actually, everybody wrote it," said Earl. "I wrote the beginning. Here's what I did: *bang-bang-bang-bang*. I wrote that. Nick said, 'Just go *bang*.' I said, 'What do you mean, just go *bang*?' So I went *bang*. And he said, 'That's right, just do that for a while.'"

That essentially was the unofficial beginning of the rehearsals for *Fool for the City* in 1974.

But Earl and Jameson wanted to find a place quieter than a soundproof basement in Long Island to start recording the album, so they rented a station wagon, put some drums, a couple of guitars, and a bass in the back and hit the road again. They arrived in Sharon, Vermont, a small town of about 1,500 people in Windsor County, and found a place called Suntreader Studios.

"We got about halfway through the recording session — on 'Slow Ride' actually — and the power went out," said Earl. "So we went out and did about three or four weeks' worth of dates and then came back — they got the power back on — and we picked up where we left off. I just started playing along with the track and we finished it.

"We spent probably three or four months actually recording there. It was terrific. Nick Jameson is a very talented producer, engineer, and musician."

In a small Vermont town there aren't many things to do, which proved to be beneficial to the band's efforts to produce a quality album.

"We weren't distracted by going out. I had some time off in between. I'd get like three or four tracks down and the rest of the guys would start doing some overdub stuff so I could go fishing or whatever I wanted to do. And vice-versa. I would do some basic tracks while the others would rest up a bit. It was really a lot of fun making that record," said Earl.

It was Earl's fondness for fishing that would eventually put the finishing touches on *Fool for the City*.

"Everybody went home after we finished most of the album and Nick and I stayed behind," said Earl. "My contribution at that point was that I made us cups of tea and got the cheese and biscuits. And I packed the drums up."

Jameson finished mixing "Slow Ride" and another track, "Save Your Loving (For Me)," written by Price and

Peverett, at Suntreader Studios before heading back home to New York.

"We drove back down from Sharon at about five in the morning and we'd been up all night the night before finishing the mixing," said Earl. "We wanted to get back and play this for Paul Fishkin, the president of Bearsville Records.

"We were pretty whacked, and I'm driving, doing about 75 m.p.h. This was the era of 55 m.p.h. About a quarter mile in front of us were some of New Hampshire's finest blocking the road. We opened up all the windows in the station wagon and hoped that it would all just sort of blow away.

"They were looking for people coming in from Canada for some reason. I pulled up to the roadblock and said, 'What's up, officer?' And he said, 'You were driving a bit quick.' I said, 'I'm sorry, I didn't get much sleep last night and we're on our way back to New York.' And he took one look at us, and he said, 'Be careful.' I said, 'Thank you.' So off we went."

The rest of the trip back to New York can best be described as the epitome of a slow ride.

Bearsville Records, founded in 1970 by Albert Grossman, had, among others, Todd Rundgren on its roster. Bearsville would release the album *Fool for the City* on Sept. 15, 1975.

"We got down to Bearsville and we played 'Slow Ride' and 'Save Your Loving' for Paul," said Earl. "He said, 'You can't put out 'Slow Ride' as a single. They [the radio stations] won't play it.'"

The original version of "Slow Ride" on the album was eight minutes and fourteen seconds long, longer than a conventional single.

"But we said, 'This is the single. This is the song.' And Paul said, 'You can't do it.' And we said, 'Fuck you, we're putting it out as a single.'

"It's actually the only time in Foghat's career that we insisted on a single. And also we refused to edit the song down," said Earl. "What happened was the radio stations edited it anyway, so we eventually did a radio version of it. But that was the only song we felt that strongly about as a single. And we were right and other people were wrong."

"Slow Ride" became the band's top single, reaching No. 20 on the Billboard Hot 100 chart.

The title track for the album was also released as a single and the band decided to call the album *Fool for the City* because, according to Earl, all the band members were living in suburban Long Island at the time.

When it came time to decide on an album cover, Earl's affinity for fishing was the inspiration.

"I used to carry rods in the car wherever I went," said Earl. "And Nick came up with the idea of going into New York. It [the song 'Fool for the City'] was basically written about New York.

"So we went into the city early one Sunday morning and went down into the Village and pulled up a manhole cover. I sat on a crate and dropped a line down the manhole," said Earl.

It was early in the morning, so there was virtually nobody on the street. Except for a couple of New York cops.

"And they said, 'Hey! Do you have a fishing license?' And I sort of looked up and said, 'Oh, shit.' And they both started laughing," said Earl. "Then they said, 'What the fuck are you guys doing?' We said, 'We're doing an album cover for a record.' So they put some handcuffs on me and we took some pictures of them dragging me away. But those didn't make it on the album cover.

"New York cops are the best. They're usually worried about rapes and murders and not a bunch of rockers pulling up manhole covers," said Earl.

The back of the album attracted some attention on the street that day as well — from the neighborhood residents. The back cover photo features the band members crowded around Earl fishing in the manhole; a young girl named Robin, who happened to be the daughter of the band's manager; and an older couple, with the man holding a can of 7-Up and scowling at the photographer.

"After the cops left, the neighborhood people came out to see what we were doing. I explained to them that I was fishing. There are some pretty large cockroaches in there [the New York sewer system]," said Earl. "I don't think the old guy had put his teeth in that day. That's why he has that look on his face."

Of the other songs on the album, Earl said that "Terraplane Blues," written by Robert Johnson, an American blues singer who died in 1938, stands out for him.

"You have to be careful when you're treading into Robert Johnson's shoes and what you do with his songs, but I really liked the way we handled that tune," said Earl. "Once again, Nick said, 'Just go *bang*, Rog. Just beat the drums as hard as you can.' Then Nick came and played bass, and Dave seemed to like the idea, so he joined in. So that's how that one started.

"'Terraplane Blues' is one of my favorites. We never played it onstage when Dave and Rod were alive, but we play it now. It's a lot of fun to play."

Despite Foghat's early reputation as a band of road warriors, Earl said he loved getting up every day and playing onstage each night.

"I had a great time. I loved it. I got what I wished for. I started playing when I was 13; I joined my first band when I was 17. It's really all I ever wanted to do. I joined Savoy Brown and didn't get paid for the first six weeks. But I hung in there. It's what I've always wanted to do," he said.

And Foghat's run in the 1970s was particularly memorable for Earl.

"There was a lot of great stuff in the 1970s. I go back to the mid-'60s through the mid-'70s, where I thought there was a really creative time for rock and roll music," he said. "There were a lot of great bands around and the music was great. The bands treated their music like it was something special."

Hotcakes and hayseeds

Flat as a Pancake
Head East

They were small-town guys from the Midwest, working hard to hone their skills on the local bar circuit. Then in 1975, virtually overnight, Head East's album *Flat as a Pancake* became a hit, and they found themselves opening for Jethro Tull.

It was the band's first time being in the "find your seat with the beat" position, an insider industry term used to describe how the opening band starts to play as fans are still getting to their seats for the headliner.

No problems, right?

Well, there was one problem. And it was a big one. Jethro Tull frontman, Ian Anderson, was a Brit who was rumored to hate American bands. And the guys from Head East didn't know that.

"It was the first major tour we were ever on and it was going to be a tour that went across the country," said John Schlitt, lead singer for the band, which also included Roger Boyd, Steve Huston, Mike Somerville, and Dan Birney.

"We were told to do exactly what they say, don't rock any boats, be happy with what they give you. So we did," said Schlitt.

The first two shows were in Detroit's Cobo Hall, which seats approximately 10,000, and each night was a sellout. It was an era when there was a PA system onstage, and another above the stage. The opening act

173

would only be projected through the onstage PA system, while the headliner played through both systems. It was done that way so the opening act never sounded as big as the headliner.

"We understood that. We understood that the headliners had paid their dues. And when they opened the doors, we had a half-hour," said Schlitt. "So we had a half-hour to do our thing, and we kicked rear end. But the minute our time was up, we were off the stage. We did exactly what we were told to do. We thought it was great, we thought it was gonna work out, this touring stuff."

So Head East did a few shows opening for Jethro Tull, partied with the crew, and everybody seemed happy.

Everyone but Ian Anderson, apparently.

By the time the tour reached the Quad Cities — the four towns of Moline and Rock Island in Illinois, and Davenport and Bettendorf in Iowa, separated by the Mississippi River — Head East was essentially back on its Midwestern home turf, and the band members wanted to do well on this big tour "at home."

"Back then we had a car and a two-ton truck and we had to do all the driving. And we had to drive overnight. We were a little tired but we wanted to make sure we did well there," said Schlitt.

"So we pulled up a little early for the load-in and the stage manager said, 'What are you guys doing here?' We said, 'We know we're a little early, but we thought we'd get unloaded and out of your way.' And he said, 'No, you guys got kicked off the tour.' We said, 'We did? Why?' And he said 'Ian Anderson called [Premier Booking, the agents for the tour] and said that he wanted you guys off the show or he wasn't touring.'"

Dejected, the band members headed back to their hotel.

"I'm in the hotel and I'm overlooking the hall that we were supposed to be playing in and thinking, 'Well, that was a short career,'" said Schlitt.

It turns out that it wasn't all that short a career for Head East, even though the band's debut album, *Flat as a Pancake*, only reached No. 126 on Billboard's Pop Albums chart. It featured the group's highest charting single, "Never Been Any Reason," which reached No. 68 on the Billboard chart.

But the album was unique in that it lingered on the charts as it played in different regions. When it first hit in the Midwest it got a lot of airplay, but by the time it started moving back down the charts there, it became popular in a different region of the country.

Head East is the story of small-town kids who had a vision and weren't afraid to go for it. They came out of Champaign, Illinois in 1969, and hit the college tour circuit as a cover band.

Schlitt graduated from college in 1973, the band took a few years to rebuild, and they began touring the circuit of clubs in Illinois, Indiana, Wisconsin, and Michigan, playing six, and sometimes seven, nights a week.

"It was a great learning field. If you were lucky enough to be part of that, it was a lot of work, but it gave you a lot of opportunity to hone your talents," said Schlitt.

By 1975, the band decided to stop being a cover band and start doing original material.

"I'll tell you what, we had some good writers. I finally got in the mode of it a little bit, but with Michael [Somerville] and Steve [Huston], especially those two guys, they started to write some pretty decent stuff," said Schlitt. "It got to a point where we'd play in clubs and you'd have club owners going, 'We don't want anything original, we want all copy stuff.' So we'd go in there and say, 'Here's a song from Three Dog Night called 'Never

Been Any Reason.' And they didn't care because the crowd loved it.

"It was fun. A lot of work. A lot of heartache because it was a lot of time away from home, but it was what we did. It was a real adventure," he said.

Instead of putting out a demo tape like many bands at the time were doing, Head East decided to put out a demo record on its own label and produce it themselves.

They found a little studio in South Pekin, Illinois, a town of about 1,000 people in central Illinois about a half-hour from Peoria, Mike Somerville's hometown.

Golden Voice Recording Co. was pretty much out in the middle of corn country. It was owned by a local guy, Jerry Milam, who would go on to become well known for building high-class home music studios that featured some of the latest technology of the era.

"We didn't know any better. We were just kids that played these 10 songs over and over again, so we knew them in our sleep," said Schlitt. "So it wasn't like we needed a lot of fancy gear; we just went in and did it. We produced it ourselves. I remember four of us standing at the board running the tape and doing the master shift of the sliders, each one of us having the responsibility of two or three sliders at a certain time. We were just kids having fun."

"When John and the guys cut *Flat as a Pancake*, I was there," said Milam. "I was working out of the back of the building; the recording studio was in the front. I was overseeing the sessions and keeping the equipment running. But I wasn't sitting at the console doing every recording."

Milam's studio became the go-to studio for Midwest bands, especially those out of Champaign, Illinois, and especially those that were being managed by Irving Azoff. Since singer-songwriter Dan Fogelberg was from nearby Peoria, Illinois, Golden Voice was also the site of Fogelberg's first recordings.

Golden Voice Recording Co. was located in South Pekin, Illinois, and was used by the band Head East to record its debut album *Flat as a Pancake* in 1975. (Photo courtesy of Jerry and Mary Ann Milam/Golden Voice Recording Co.)

And Azoff, who was managing Fogelberg at the time, would eventually move to Los Angeles in the early 1970s and manage several big-name artists including The Eagles, Van Halen, Steely Dan, and Lindsay Buckingham of Fleetwood Mac.

"Irving Azoff was the kingpin for all the Midwest bands," said Milam. "He was sending bands our way at quite a rate because he was trying to get recording contracts for them."

Although Milam didn't sit in with Head East during the recording of *Flat as a Pancake*, he did a little advance work that may have helped the sound on that album.

"I had modified the recording console just before that album was cut," said Milam. "I had run some experiments on some things because I was trying to achieve a certain kind of sound. So I went in and modified my entire recording console module by module just before *Flat as a Pancake* was cut. I don't know if it helped make the thing a seller or not, but everybody liked the sound that came out of that. Head East were the first guys to cut on the modified recording console after I did the work on it."

Hoping to achieve a specific sound, Jerry Milam, owner of Gold Voice Recording Co., had modified the recording console just before *Flat as a Pancake* was recorded.
(Photo courtesy of Jerry and Mary Ann Milam/Golden Voice Recording Co.)

Head East members had decided to call the album *Flat as a Pancake* long before it was recorded. When the band retooled in 1973, band members had spent some time in Colorado rebuilding and refocusing.

"We came back and we were driving from Champaign to Bloomington, Illinois. And we were reminiscing about Colorado and all this and we were looking out over the prairie of the Midwest and somebody said, 'Man, that is flat as a pancake.' Then somebody else said, 'You know what, we need to call our first album *Flat as a Pancake*. At the time, it was like, yeah, sure. And sure enough, we remembered that conversation. And our first album was called *Flat as a Pancake*," said Schlitt.

The band cut 2,000 copies of *Flat as a Pancake* in 1974 on a label they called Pyramid Records. Band members took loans from family members and friends to pay for the cost of producing 2,000 albums. The record ended up costing the band between $13,000 and $14,000, which included recording time, the 2,000 albums, and about 800 eight-track cassettes.

And band members sent copies to every radio station in the middle part of the country. The song "Never Been Any Reason" started to get some air time on Midwest college radio stations, so the band decided to send the album to bigger promoters.

The record landed in the lap of Contemporary Productions, which at the time was one of the, if not the, biggest promoter in the Midwest. And Contemporary Productions officials were looking for new talent to manage.

"And they picked up this record, and the owner listened to it and goes, 'Oh my gosh, this is a hit record. This is a hit record!'" said Schlitt.

From there, the record made it to KSHE 95 in St. Louis, the No. 2 breakout station in the country at the time. And then to Y-102 in Kansas City. All of a sudden, Head East had the No. 1 requested album, *Flat as a Pancake*, and the No.1 requested single, "Never Been Any Reason," in the Midwest.

John Schlitt was the lead singer of Head East when it recorded
Flat as a Pancake in 1975.
(Photo courtesy of John Schlitt)

"I was the one handling the business side of Head
East at the time and I'm getting calls from distributors
wanting 10,000 copies of *Flat as a Pancake* as quickly as
possible," said Schlitt. "It took me six months to get 2,000
copies!

"Do you realize what kind of a dream come true
that is? After working your tail off and getting rejections
from everybody saying, 'When you get big time, we'll talk
to you' and all of a sudden - bam! - you're big time. The
big boys were talking. And these big boys had
connections."

Head East was now in a position to choose its own
record company, and band members chose A&M
Records.

"We chose it because it was the classiest record
company in the industry. And it only took a few artists,"
said Schlitt.

A&M Records re-released *Flat as a Pancake* in 1975 under its own banner.

The cover of the album features an orange and yellow checkerboard pattern surrounding a photo of a single pancake on a plate covered with butter and syrup. But it's the back of the album that fans — and Schlitt — seem to remember the most.

The back cover features a photo of the band members sitting in a little diner eating pancakes. The photo was taken in what was then called the RiteWay Diner in Olivette, Missouri, near St. Louis. It shows Schlitt feeding a bite of pancakes to Boyd.

"I hate that back cover. I hate that picture more than any other picture I've ever taken, I think. That's got to be one of the worst rock pictures I've ever seen. But everybody loves it," said Schlitt.

"And those pancakes, they had been sitting there for hours. It was the first major photo shoot that we had ever done and it lasted forever. Those pancakes were ice cold. Every once in a while they'd put a couple of hot ones on top and then we were supposed to act like we were eating them. Yeah, right. Pancakes that had been sitting around for four hours. No, thank you.

"All I could think was that this was the first picture people are ever gonna see of us and we look like a bunch of hayseeds. Look at us. It wasn't cool at all," he said. "But you got to understand, I'm a lead singer, I'm very insecure. I want to look cool no matter what."

Head East recorded five more albums after releasing *Flat as a Pancake*. Birney and Somerville left the band in 1980, and Schlitt's tenure with the group ended around the same time as he fell into drug dependency.

After Schlitt got clean, he joined the contemporary Christian rock group Petra in the mid-1980s. But he has fond memories of his days with Head East.

"It was a very rare experience that very few people get to go through. Think about it. Five kids on their own, had to borrow the money, spent next to nothing, and were successful. And that record opened the door for us that fulfilled a musician's dream for years," said Schlitt.

"In my case, I blew it [by succumbing to the drugs]. It finally started burning me out and I was away from my family so much I started to feel like I was a prisoner. You forget that the dream sometimes costs you.

"But to be a musician with that kind of drive, we were very serious about what we wanted to do. And man, when it hit, we rode it, and we rode it for a long time," he said. "I was very proud of Head East."

Pictured is some of the equipment that recording artists used at Golden Voice Recording Co. in the 1970s.
(Photo courtesy of Jerry and Mary Ann Milam/Golden Voice Recording Co.)

It didn't fail for your ears

The Higher They Climb, the Harder They Fall
and
Home Is Where the Heart Is
David Cassidy

*I*f it were not for Captain & Tennille and David Cassidy, Barry Manilow might never have recorded the Grammy Award-winning song, "I Write the Songs."

Or so said the song's writer, Bruce Johnston of the Beach Boys.

The iconic classic was one of Manilow's three No. 1 hits during the 1970s and won a Grammy Award for Song of the Year in 1977. And the path the song took to iconic status features several connecting threads of classic rock-and-roll history from the 1970s.

Cassidy was just coming off a successful run as Keith Partridge in the wildly popular television series *The Partridge Family*, which aired from 1970 through 1974. He was a teen idol sensation, and girls went absolutely *Beatles-type-of-freakout-crazy* when Cassidy appeared in public.

Given the fact that his character on *The Partridge Family* had a gee-whiz comedic aspect to it, some in the music industry didn't at first recognize the high level of Cassidy's musical abilities.

But Johnston wasn't one of the doubters. David Cassidy wanted to be the "real" David Cassidy — not

185

TV's Keith Partridge — and Johnston recognized that right away. So Johnston agreed to co-produce, with Cassidy, his first two solo albums for RCA Records, *The Higher They Climb, the Harder They Fall* in 1975, and *Home Is Where the Heart Is* in 1976.

"I think one thing people don't know is that David played really great electric guitar. You can kind of play guitar onstage and get by and that's cool, but he played on his solo album tracks," said Johnston, the only Beach Boy who won a Grammy Award for Song of the Year.

"We had world-class musicians and vocalists recording with him and he really held his own in the studio. David worked extremely hard on both of his solo albums."

Johnston and his longtime friend and production partner, Terry Melcher (son of actress/singer Doris Day), had a worldwide production deal with RCA Records. Johnston and Melcher had the option of signing artists to the RCA label and also producing artists already signed to RCA. In fact, Johnston said, they had a really generous production deal with the label.

"I think with all the 'light' albums David recorded as a member of The Partridge family, he was probably dying to create and record something serious," said Johnston. "And I was really the right guy to work with for him because *I got it*. I could just tell David would make great albums, given the chance."

Johnston called Cassidy a "hands-on artist" with his first two solo albums for RCA, much the same way Frank Sinatra was with his albums.

"Sinatra would pick his songs and get very involved with the arrangements and the back-in-the-day production. He probably should have had a production credit on all his recordings," said Johnston. "David just wanted to do something really wonderful, and I think his two solo albums really hit the mark. But I don't think the

186

general public, or even the label, were thinking that way. I think they were just wanting the former *Partridge Family* teen idol to now become a solo 'pop' artist, churning out endless hit singles."

Pictured is longtime Beach Boys keyboardist and vocalist Bruce Johnston, left, and 1970s teen idol, television star and recording artist David Cassidy, right. Johnston produced Cassidy's first two solo albums, *The Higher They Climb, the Harder They Fall* and *Home is Where the Heart Is* in the mid-1970s. (Photo courtesy of Bruce Johnston)

And that's where choosing "I Write the Songs" came into play. It was Johnston's song, and Cassidy wanted it on *The Higher They Climb, the Harder They Fall* because he needed the album to have a hit song.

"I'm surprised he selected it, as it seemed like, at best, just a lateral music move. I've always kind of wondered if David thought, 'Maybe I better record it because I know that it could be a hit.'

"It's kind of like insurance," said Johnston. "I know David always says that he was the first one to record it, but it really was Captain & Tennille."

"I Write the Songs" appeared on Captain & Tennille's 1975 debut, multi-platinum album, *Love Will Keep Us Together.* Their album includes another Johnston-written song, "Disney Girls," as well as the Brian Wilson song, "God Only Knows."

Johnston likened Cassidy's decision to record "I Write the Songs" and to include it on his album to Capitol Records' decision to include the song "Sloop John B" on the 1966 Beach Boys album *Pet Sounds*, considered to be Brian Wilson's greatest studio masterpiece.

"Al Jardine convinced Brian to record 'Sloop John B' in 1965, and Al laid out a great road map/arrangement for Brian," said Johnston.

The 1965 track for the recording was in the Capitol Records vault for a short time when in 1966 the "Sloop John B" vocals were recorded. Later on, the song was included on *Pet Sounds*.

"Do you think 'Sloop John B' belongs on that album? No! What does it have to do with that album? Nothing, even though it's a really great recording. Capitol Records convinced Brian to include 'Sloop John B' on the *Pet Sounds* album," said Johnston.

And Johnston believes that Cassidy had a similar "label" mindset when he chose to record "I Write the Songs" for *The Higher They Climb, the Harder They Fall*.

"David was making this really great first solo album, but I kind of think he, too, was looking for a little song insurance," said Johnston. "Like 'Sloop John B,' here is the insurance song, or so he [and RCA Records] thought.

"Now we have a very cool first solo album — *The Higher They Climb, the Harder They Fall* — concept, but the album has one weak track and it's "I Write the Songs;" but I'm sure David didn't think of it that way then. It was well-recorded and sung, but I always felt that it contradicted the 'serious' direction of David's album."

"I Write the Songs" reached No. 11 for Cassidy in England, but the Manilow version would reach No. 1 in the U.S. and become Manilow's signature song.

"At the end of the day, I remember David pushing RCA to focus on 'Get It Up for Love' instead of 'I Write

188

the Songs' as the single off *The Higher They Climb, the Harder They Fall* album."

As an aside, Johnston said that he didn't write "I Write the Songs" for Brian Wilson, as some have suggested over the years.

"If you ever read that I wrote 'I Write the Songs,' about Brian Wilson, please disregard it. I wrote that song as a hymn to God for being the spirit of creativity in all of us. It gets me nuts when people say I wrote it for Brian Wilson," said Johnston.

When it came time to choose an album cover for *The Higher They Climb, the Harder They Fall*, Cassidy once again made the call. The cover features Cassidy apparently flying upward in the sky while adoring fans look at him from the ground.

"It was his idea for the album cover. My only input on that was applause," said Johnston. "I'm just an artist masquerading as a producer. I get all that stuff. I saw right where he was coming from. I was talking like a big brother to David, artistically.

"I loved that cover. Did David's first solo album commercially achieve massive success? Not really. It did OK; it sold enough. Artistically for David, did it personally achieve what he was hoping for? I'd like to think so," said Johnston.

The follow-up album, *Home Is Where the Heart Is,* was also co-produced by Cassidy and Johnston. It featured songwriting and vocal contributions from Gerry Beckley of the band America, which also had established itself as one of the top recording and touring bands by the mid-1970s.

Cassidy and Beckley co-wrote two songs, "Take This Heart" and "Bedtime," for the album. Cassidy shared writing credits with musician/songwriter Bill House on four songs, and Cassidy also cut the Paul and Linda McCartney-penned song, "Tomorrow" for the record.

"Who wouldn't want to work with Gerry Beckley?" said Johnston.

"And I had enough sense to never get in the way. Sometimes you have to really assert yourself as a producer, but David wasn't blowing it in the studio. He was like an actor who gets to direct his first film. I didn't have to step in very much. There are great session players on that album and I happen to really love [the band] America," said Johnston.

Cassidy also had good sense on *Home Is Where the Heart Is,* about who he wanted playing and singing with him. Session musicians like King Errisson on percussion, Jesse Ed Davis on guitar, and Stephen Ross on keyboards provided support. And for vocalists, Cassidy chose an all-star lineup. In addition to Beckley and Johnston on vocals, Cassidy surrounded himself with Carl Wilson of The Beach Boys, Richie Furay of Buffalo Springfield and Poco, Dewey Bunnell of America, and Howard Kaylan and Mark Volman (Flo & Eddie) of The Turtles, among others.

"It was really fun to work with all those great session players and vocalists. And David wasn't making any mistakes by who he called up to back him in the studio," said Johnston, who compared the talent of the vocalists to the cast of the 1963 film, *It's a Mad, Mad, Mad, Mad World*, which featured a host of A-list actors, including Spencer Tracy, Milton Berle, Sid Caesar, Buddy Hackett, Mickey Rooney, and Jonathan Winters.

"David wasn't doing it for celebrity wallpaper. He listened to [the] music and determined, 'Here is what I think I should do,'" said Johnston.

When it comes to *The Higher They Climb, the Harder They Fall* and *Home Is Where the Heart Is*, Johnston reiterates the two things he originally said about Cassidy: that in that mid-1970s, people did not realize that Cassidy was a serious musician, and that he was trying to achieve a high personal standard of musicianship with his two solo albums.

"With David Cassidy, it doesn't matter if David hit home runs or failed artistically because David Cassidy did not fail for your ears. He can look back over his life and realize that he had a shot at doing something that he wanted to do, instead of just taking songs off the rack and having a TV show to back him up.

"I'm for the artist realizing what they should be doing and then achieving it in the studio," said Johnston.

The author interviews Bruce Johnston of The Beach Boys prior to a 1986 concert in Rockford, Illinois.

Flying potatoes and white pants don't mix

Scheherazade and Other Stories
Renaissance

It was challenging to be one of The King's Singers in the mid-1970s if Annie Haslam was in the vicinity. The King's Singers, a British a cappella group whose popularity peaked in the 1970s and early 1980s, were known to wear red jackets and white pants for their performances.

It wasn't out of the question in that era to see The King's Singers hanging around Abbey Road Studios in London, which is where they crossed paths with Haslam, lead singer for Renaissance, one afternoon in May 1975.

Renaissance was recording a portion of its next album, *Scheherazade and Other Stories*, at Abbey Road Studios. In between recording sessions, band members would grab lunch in the studio's restaurant, located in the basement.

"It was fantastic, the food was great. English homemade cooking," said Haslam.

One afternoon, Haslam and Renaissance bandmate John Tout went to the restaurant and found themselves at a table near where The King's Singers were having lunch.

"I was with John and he was sitting opposite of me and right behind him were [The] King's Singers, with their white pants on," said Haslam. "Well, it was toward the end of the lunchtime, so the roasted potatoes were

getting pretty hard. I tried to put my fork and knife into
this potato, but it was too hard, and it flew off my plate,
over John's shoulder and into the lap of one of The King's
Singers, right onto his white pants. I could never have
done that in a million years. You know, there are just
certain things that stick in your mind."

Aside from the flying potato, there are some other
memories that Haslam associates with the recording of
Scheherazade and Other Stories. One was that Haslam
had just started dating Roy Wood, co-founder of bands
The Move, Electric Light Orchestra, and Wizzard.
Another was that as soon as Renaissance was finished
recording the album, Haslam had surgery on her left ear.

But her most compelling memory is the excitement
of the era.

"There was a lot of emotion and a lot of drama at
that time," said Haslam. "But it was extremely exciting to
be in the studio, recording with the orchestra and choir.
Oh my God, it was just unbelievable.

"In fact, Paul McCartney was in one day and he
needed to borrow a tambourine — he needed a certain
kind — so we lent him a tambourine. It was a very
exciting time, it really was. There were always famous
people coming and going."

Renaissance, which combined progressive rock
with classical and symphonic influences, traces its origins
to 1969 when The Yardbirds disbanded. Keith Reif and
Jim McCarty decided to form a new group that would
combine rock, folk, and classical forms of music.

By 1971, Renaissance had undergone several
incarnations and Reif and McCarty were gone.
Renaissance re-emerged with lead singer Haslam,
guitarists/composers Michael Dunford and John Tout,
Neil Korner, Terry Crowe, and Terry Slade. By 1973, the
band had again gone through several line-up changes,
when Terrance Sullivan and Jon Camp joined and helped

take Renaissance to the next level by concentrating on the United States market.

The band left Sovereign Records in 1974 — it had joined Sovereign in 1972 — and signed with Miles Copeland's BTM (British Talent Management) label. A larger budget allowed Renaissance to take on more of an orchestral sound, as evidenced by the group's first album for the new label, *Turn of the Cards,* in 1974. That was followed by the release of *Scheherazade and Other Stories* in 1975.

"It's difficult for me to say which song or which album is a favorite because I love them all," said Haslam. "Why wouldn't I? There are some great songs: 'Mother Russia,' 'Running Hard,' 'Ocean Gypsy,' [and] 'Trip to the Fair.'

"But 'Scheherazade' is a masterpiece; there's no doubt about that," she said. "I'm not saying it's *the* masterpiece. I think the song 'Mother Russia' is a masterpiece — the way it's structured, the atmosphere in it — the words are very poignant.

"I think there is more than one masterpiece, but I think that maybe 'Scheherazade' is the No. 1 masterpiece."

Haslam said that fans responded positively when *Scheherazade and Other Stories* was released, and that the band was thrilled to be asked to perform the album at Carnegie Hall in New York.

"That was quite an experience," she said. "We were there for three nights and we had a choir onstage. Even the rehearsals with the choir were quite stunning. I could barely sing when I was onstage."

For the shows, Haslam had special dresses made by Thea Porter, a famous dress designer at the time, who had a boutique in London. Miles Copeland, the band's manager, was the one who took Haslam to Porter's boutique.

The Vinyl Dialogues

"That was an amazing experience as well, going into her place and seeing and feeling all the clothes and fabrics from all those Middle Eastern countries," said Haslam. "She made me two dresses, one to wear for the princess scene in *Scheherazade*, which I wore at the beginning of the show. Then I would go offstage and there was a musical piece before the festival, and then I would come back in this light peacock blue dress."

Although Haslam has become an accomplished painter over the years, she hadn't yet started painting when the album cover was designed for *Scheherazade and Other Stories*. But she liked it.

"I think it's beautiful," she said. "I think we were maybe expecting something a little grander at the time, but we accepted it."

Even though Renaissance has historically been described as a progressive rock band, Haslam disagrees.

"Most people say that, but I don't think it really fits us. Progressive rock is usually a bit heavier. I've always described us as classical rock or symphonic rock. To somebody that has never heard us, that gives them an idea what to expect."

Haslam said that she always had a sense that the music of Renaissance was special for people, especially those in the United States.

"It's like classical music to me; it's timeless," said Haslam. "It never changes. It's always been that way and it's wonderful. It's set apart from everything else, and I think our music is that way as well because it kept that element going."

The untimely death of guitarist and composer Michael Dunford in 2012 gave Haslam pause and caused her to question whether that was the end of Renaissance. They had been singing together since 1971.

"It was difficult, and I wasn't really quite sure if I should carry on," said Haslam. "And then I knew that

196

Mickey — I used to call him Mickey and it used to drive him crazy — would want me to carry on. And the fans wanted it.

"It's the music, really. The music is so special and so timeless, and as long as I can still sing it and the fans are there, then we should carry on."

The 'No Breakfast After 10:30 a.m.' rule

Year of the Cat
Al Stewart

*C*ongratulations, you're a rock star! And no, you can't have breakfast.

That was Al Stewart's realization in 1976, on the day he found out that his seventh studio album, *Year of the Cat*, had made it into the Top 10.

It was his first Top 10 album and, at the time, Stewart was staying at a Holiday Inn in Kentucky, across the Mississippi River from Cincinnati, Ohio. His manager had called from Los Angeles to inform him of the good news. To celebrate, Stewart decided to go down to the hotel restaurant and eat breakfast. But as is the case with many musicians, they oftentimes stay up late and play music, which means they don't climb out of bed too early the next morning.

Such was the case that day when Stewart went looking for breakfast around 11 a.m., and walked into an empty hotel restaurant.

"The staff pointed to the clock and said, 'We stopped serving breakfast at 10:30 a.m.' And there was no one in this restaurant except me," said Stewart.

The cook went back to reading a magazine and chatting with the waitress.

"So I said, 'You're not doing anything else; can you make me some breakfast?'" said Stewart.

Apparently not. The staff was strictly adhering to the "No Breakfast After 10:30 a.m." rule.

Stewart pointed to a rack behind the counter that held a row of one-serving boxes of dry cereal.

"Look, all you have to do is put your hand up there, take down a box of cereal, pass it over to me, and give me a bowl of milk and I'll do the rest myself," said Stewart.

"Nope, it's after 10:30 a.m. and you can't have breakfast," insisted the cook.

"I was thinking to myself, 'I've got a record in the Top 10 and there are people all over America who are digging it. I could probably walk down the street singing 'Year of the Cat' and someone would invite me in and give me breakfast.' And this guy, whose job it is to make me breakfast, won't let me have it," said Stewart.

For a moment, Stewart said, he considered taking a $100 bill out of his pocket, slamming it down on the counter, and yelling, "Give me some breakfast!"

"But I thought, 'That is such rock-'n-roll behavior.' So I just went somewhere else and found something to eat," he said.

Unfortunately for Stewart, he was on the road touring during the entire time that *Year of the Cat* stayed in the Top 10; by the time he got back to Los Angeles, the album had fallen out of the Top 10 and was headed back down the charts.

"I kind of missed out on all the parties and the groupies and everything," he said.

Stewart said a lot of people thought *Year of the Cat* was his first album, but it was indeed his seventh studio effort. His first four albums were released only in Britain.

He said he did what everybody else was doing at the time, and that was writing love songs.

"It grew tedious, even for my audience. I mean, I'd written an 18-minute love song and I figured once you've done that, you've pretty much said it all," said Stewart.

The Scottish-born Stewart was part of the British folk revival of the 1960s and 1970s. But he became known for writing folk-rock songs that featured characters and events from history. His fifth album, *Past, Present and Future*, was an album of historical songs, and he said he did that purely for himself because he liked history.

"I thought, 'No one is going to buy this,' and it outsold the first four albums put together," he said.

His sixth album, *Modern Times*, actually made the Top 30 on both sides of the Atlantic and sold 150,000 copies. So by the time Stewart recorded and released *Year of the Cat*, he was fairly certain that he was headed for a Top 20 album. But then the title track became a hit single, and everything changed.

"I obviously didn't think I would have a hit single because I never had one to that point," said Stewart. "But I thought it would make the Top 20 and I thought it would probably sell a quarter of a million copies and that sounded really good to me.

The thing I never saw coming was that it would be a hit single, which, of course, made it sell a lot more than that."

One of the unique aspects of *Year of the Cat* wasn't unique at all for Stewart. On several albums leading up to *Year of the Cat*, Stewart recorded all of the music before writing any of the lyrics. It was kind of a high-wire act for Stewart, because a lot of the money that went into making an album in those days went to the studio musicians. And for *Year of the Cat*, Stewart had a complete record with no vocals on it.

"If you go into the studio with a blues band, the lead guitar player will usually do six or eight or ten solos," said Stewart. "They'll pick the best one and maybe they'll

edit it together. I thought, 'Why can't you do that in
reverse?'"

Stewart had all the backing tracks and if a song
needed four verses, he'd write 12 verses so he could pick
and choose the ones he liked best. Sometimes, he'd write
four sets of lyrics on completely different subjects.

"Even 'Year of the Cat' was called 'Foot of the
Stage,' about a comedian who committed suicide. I just
basically wrote lots and lots of words and then sat down
and said, 'Which ones do I want to use?' To this day, I
don't know if I picked the best ones, but I picked the ones
I liked at the time. I made all those records that way, with
the backing tracks first."

Year of the Cat was recorded at the already
renowned Abbey Road Studios. Although it was primitive
by today's standards, the Beatles had made the place
famous and it had a unique sense of history about it.

"You get that sense of history; you can't avoid it,"
said Stewart. "You're in a room and someone says, 'They
recorded "A Day in the Life" in here.' And you're like,
'Boy, this is pretty important.' I ran into Linda McCartney
in there one day. You pass people in the hall and say, 'Oh
my God, that's Allan Clarke from The Hollies!'"

Of the songs on the record, Stewart said that
"Flying Sorcery" and "On the Border" are two of his
favorites. Whereas "On the Border" was written in about
15 minutes — "about as fast as my pen could move across
the paper" — it was "Flying Sorcery" that fascinated
Stewart, he said, because it went through so many
changes.

"It took a long time. I think I was reading a book
on World War I aircraft at the time and I was hung up on
the word 'aileron' [a part of the tail wing of an aircraft that
helps a pilot steer a plane].

"And I got everything else in the damn song but I
just couldn't squeeze that word in. In fact, I think the

whole motivation for doing a flying song was to use the word 'aileron.'

That kind of pissed me off for about 30 years, and finally in 2005 when I put out the album *A Beach Full of Shells*, I wrote another flying song just so I could put in the word 'aileron.'"

As for the title track of *Year of the Cat*, Stewart was not fond of the saxophone that's a distinct part of that song. It was the record's producer, Alan Parsons, who suggested the saxophone for that song.

"I always thought saxophones sounded like wounded cows," said Stewart. "I've never been fond of them. Beyond that, I can tolerate them on Duane Eddy records because it works. My real objection was that the saxophone has nothing to do with folk-rock. I always thought of it as a jazz instrument. The whole folk-rock thing is like jangling guitars — you know, The Byrds, Simon and Garfunkel — those kinds of things."

Stewart was trying to make a folk-rock record and was skeptical about using the saxophone sound, but Parsons insisted.

"Alan said, 'Well, let's put it on there and let's sleep on it,'" said Stewart. "So I did sleep on it and it still sounded like a wounded cow in the morning. But everyone else liked it, so I said fine. I guess it doesn't matter; it's only one track and it's the last track of the record and no one is going to hear it anyway."

It only became a No. 8 chart single for Stewart and he had only one other single in his career that topped it, "Time Passages," which reached No. 7 in 1978.

As for the album cover, it was designed by Storm Thorgerson, who had an art design company called Hipgnosis, based in London. The company had also designed album covers for Led Zeppelin and Pink Floyd, among other notable musicians.

So for *Year of the Cat*, as well as for other album covers produced by Hipgnosis, its personnel would listen to a few songs from the album to get a sense of what the album was trying to convey, and then the musician wouldn't see any of the process until the final design.

Al Stewart signed a copy of his 1976 album *Year of the Cat* for the author backstage at the Keswick Theatre in Glenside, PA, during a show in March 2013 where Stewart shared the bill with Dave Mason.
(Photo by Judy Morsch)

"When I first saw the *Year of the Cat* album cover, I thought it was absolutely great," said Stewart. "But I really didn't have any idea what they were going to do until I saw it."

The back of the album features a picture of Stewart in a white leisure suit, popular attire in the 1970s.

"I bought that for a wedding. I'm not really a dress-up person," said Stewart. "A friend of mine was getting married. It was 1976, so it just happened to be that

204

John Travolta era where people wore white suits. So I bought a white suit, and of course, within six months the country was all tied up with disco and it was terribly gauche to wear a white suit. It was the only suit I owned, but I don't think I ever wore it again after that photo shoot."

Even though it's been nearly 40 years since *Year of the Cat* has been released, Stewart has maintained a consistent songwriting approach during his entire career.

"I have basically two philosophies and I can tell you right now how I do this. It's not a conjuring trick," said Stewart. "There are only two things that I'm interested in when I'm writing a song: 1. Don't write about anything that anyone else has ever written about because originality is the key thing; 2. And in my way of doing things, use words that no one else uses. That way, you're absolutely bound to be original. That's how I do everything."

The walls have ears
for a hit song

Nights are Forever
England Dan & John Ford Coley

Sometimes, thin walls can be a good thing. For England Dan & John Ford Coley, thin walls were responsible for making "I'd Really Love to See You Tonight" a hit single.

Dan Seals and John Colley, performing as Colley and Wayland, signed with A&M Records in the early 1970s. But after producing three albums that failed to chart in the United States, they were released from their contract with A&M Records in 1976.

They performed under the name "Colley and Wayland" using the original spelling of Coley's last name, and Dan Seals' middle name, Wayland. But they needed a change.

And according to Coley, Jim Seals of the 1970s soft rock duo, Seals & Crofts — Dan's brother — is actually credited with the band's improved name, "England Dan & John Ford Coley."

As a child, Dan Seals was a Beatles fan and used to mimic an English accent. So Jim Seals started calling his brother "England Dan."

"If you've ever heard a Texan try to imitate anything other than a Texas accent, it's kind of comical," said Coley.

And Coley changed his name up a bit as well.

"Nobody in my lifetime has been able to pronounce my last name," said Coley. "I've been called Cooley, Cowley, Connolly, Coley, everything but Colley."

So Coley dropped one "L" from his last name and instead of using his middle name, "Edward," decided to use "Ford," after Colonel John Salmon "Rip" Ford, the last Confederate general in the Civil War to win a battle for the South in Sabine, Texas. And Jim Seals suggested that "England Dan & John Ford Coley" had the right sound and flow.

After being dropped by A&M Records, the duo kind of wandered for a year or so, not because they were lost, according to Coley, but because they were perfecting their craft in the hopes of landing another record deal. And then their manager, Susan Joseph, brought them the song, "I'd Really Love to See You Tonight," written by Mississippi-based songwriter Parker McGee.

"We really didn't want to do it," said Coley. "We thought it was more of a female song. But our manager said, 'Please try it,' so we did."

They brought in Louie Shelton, a seasoned session musician who had worked with the likes of Simon and Garfunkel, Stevie Wonder, and The Monkees. He also produced the first couple of England Dan & John Ford Coley albums, and brought in Jeff Pocaro and David Paich, later of Toto, to cut a demo tape of "I'd Really Love to See You Tonight."

Joseph then took the tape to Atlantic Records, and it made it into the office of Bob Greenberg, Vice President at Atlantic Records, where it was played for the record executive.

Greenberg was not impressed.

Immediately after the tape had been played, there was a knock on Greenberg's office door. Sitting in an adjacent room were Doug Morris and Dick Vanderbilt, executives of Big Tree Records, a subsidiary of Atlantic. Founded by Morris, he had sold Big Tree to Atlantic Records in 1974. Morris would eventually go on to become co-chairman of Atlantic before it closed its doors for good in 1980.

But at that moment, Morris and Vanderbilt were interested in "I'd Really Love to See You Tonight" because they had heard the demo tape through the thin walls of Greenberg's office.

According to the story as related to Coley by manager Susan Joseph, Morris asked Greenberg if he was interested in recording the song.

"Well, Bob, what do you think of that record? You like that? You gonna take it?" Susan Joseph recalls Morris saying to Greenberg.

"I'm sorry, I just don't think this one's got it. We're going to pass," Joseph remembered Greenberg saying. "And Morris said, 'We'll take the song.'"

The single would become the biggest hit that England Dan & John Ford Coley ever had, reaching No. 2 on the Billboard Hot 100 in 1976. It would also go on to anchor the duo's next album, *Nights are Forever*, also released in 1976. *Nights are Forever* peaked at No. 10 on the Billboard chart, and featured a title-track single, also written by McGee.

"We only had a singles deal with Atlantic, and [executives] were talking about possibly doing an album if the single took off," said Coley. "And Dan and I were kind of unhappy because we were writing songs all the time, and now some other writer [McGee] comes in and he's written the song that everybody wants.

"And then we got our first royalty check, and I was like, 'OK, where are some more songs that other people had written? I think up to that point I had made about $1.98 on the songs I had written all those years."

So Seals and Coley brought in session musicians and began building an album around "I'd Really Love to See You Tonight."

"We began to cut this thing, and the players were so great," said Coley. "Dan and I were so low-key and laid-back. I remember the drummer saying, 'Man, I just love these no pressure sessions.' He'd play something and say, 'What about this?' And we'd go, 'Yeah, that sounds good. Just do that.' The musicians, they weren't accustomed to that."

The album, produced by Kyle Lehning, was recorded at the Studio by the Pond — the home of recording engineer Lee Hazen — at Old Hickory Lake near Hendersonville, Tennessee.

Between sessions, Coley and the musicians played a lot of ping-pong, while Seals oftentimes relaxed by fishing in the lake.

"Everything just kind of came together. We had a lot of good players," said Coley.

Even Dan's brother, Jim Seals, played on the album.

"There was a good friend who we used to play with back in Texas named Shane Keister, and he and I doubled up in a band we were in. I played organ and he played piano and Dan was one of the singers.

"So when we came into town, there were certain things that I didn't want to play. And we pulled Shane in and he did such a wonderful job for us," said Coley.

Nights Are Forever became the duo's fourth studio album and its highest charter, peaking at No. 17 in the United States. Two subsequent albums, *Dowdy Ferry Farm* in 1977 and *Some Things Don't Come Easy* in 1978 broke into the Top 100. *Dowdy Ferry Farm* featured the single "It's Sad to Belong," which reached No. 21; and *Some Things Don't Come Easy* featured "We'll Never

Have to Say Goodbye," which became the band's second-best charting single, reaching No. 9.

The *Nights are Forever* album cover features Seals and Coley in mid-1970s-style leisure suits.

"Dan and I were blue jeans kind of guys, so they wanted us to wear these suits," said Coley. "And I'll be doggone if we didn't wear those suits for like two years."

Coley said there are actually two versions of the album cover. Once the album began to take off, some "alterations" were made in the cover photo of the two, and the album was re-released as sales continued to increase.

"Well, they straightened out my collar, they removed a mole off my chin, they removed a sprig of hair, and they took two pimples off Dan's face and straightened up his shirt collar," said Coley. "The record went gold, so they just straightened up a bunch of stuff on it and made it a little bit more professional."

Coley said one of the interesting comparisons about the duo made in the 1970s, was when they were compared to Seals and Crofts.

"Jimmy Seals is Dan's brother, but they were so diametrically opposed temperamentally that it was staggering," said Coley. "People would compare Dan to Dash Crofts — both were extraordinarily laid-back. Dan was one of the funniest people you'd ever want to meet in your life. He kept me laughing so much. He was also a very wise man. He was like a gentle giant. Then people would compare me to Jimmy, because Jimmy was quick-tempered and would be down your throat in a New York-minute. And I was right there with him. I've mellowed over the years, but it was really an interesting comparison."

Seals and Coley were together as a duo from 1965 to 1980, and both were practicing members of the Baha'i religion. After their breakup, they didn't communicate much for many years, possibly because their careers had taken very different paths.

Dan Seals died in 2009 after a battle with mantle cell lymphoma.

Even though Coley left the Baha'i faith and converted to Christianity, he was allowed to speak with Seals before his death.

"Dan and I didn't have much contact in the past several years, but I did talk to him the day before he died," said Coley. "We were both in the same religion for a while, so when I went back to Christianity/Judaism, they [the people around Seals] wouldn't let me talk to him because they were afraid I was going to try and convert him back or something, which I was not trying to do at all. So they kind of kept me away from him.

"But before he died, we got to talk to one another. All the things that might have happened that were not pleasant, that stuff was just tossed right out the window. I mean, it had been gone for me for about 15 years, anyway. And he was just Dan again and everything was good between us. It was good closure."

Coley said that becoming a star was never the primary goal for himself and Seals.
"We just loved playing and would go out and play everywhere," said Coley. "We really didn't look at it as going as far as it actually did. I thought probably it might last a couple of years and then I would grow up and go off and be as boring as all my friends were. It didn't work out that way. God kind of has different plans for you.

"I'm still kind of surprised when people say that we made history," said Coley. "And I go, 'OK, really?' For me, I was just having fun. I loved it. I had the best time of my life."

Defining the 'Jersey Shore Sound' with help from The Boss

I Don't Want to Go Home
Southside Johnny & the Asbury Jukes

Steven Van Zandt's direct musical lineage — ranging from The Rascals to Southside Johnny & the Asbury Jukes — claims Bruce Springsteen and the E Street Band as the connecting link.

And along the way, because of him, the "Jersey Shore Sound" was redefined.

The outcome of traveling this musical road was the 1976 Southside Johnny & the Asbury Jukes debut album, *I Don't Want to Go Home* , as well as the Jukes' second and third albums, *This Time It's for Real* in 1977 and *Hearts of Stone* in 1978.

According to Van Zandt, The Rascals were the first band in the mid-to-late-1960s that brought soul and blues influences into the rock genre.

"Not a literal interpretation, because that would require horns and a lot of background vocalists and more instrumentation, but they were the rock version of soul music," said Van Zandt. "And this made an enormous impact on us."

Southside Johnny & the Asbury Jukes were that literal translation. The band did have horns and did combine soul and rock music.

"The E Street Band, of course, had the gospel

instrumentation from Day One with the organ and the piano," said Van Zandt, who joined Springsteen's band on guitar in 1975 during its *Born to Run* tour.

"Right from the beginning, the E Street Band — once Roy [Bittan] joined and added the piano in '75 — it right away changed the format from more of a rock band to a gospel soul band. That's the instrumentation of a soul band," said Van Zandt.

So Springsteen was already leaning that way when it came to redefining the "Jersey Shore Sound" in terms of bar bands.

"The bar bands' configuration, the bar bands' sound, the bar bands' music, literally changed its definition with Southside Johnny & the Asbury Jukes," said Van Zandt. "Before that, bar bands were strictly Top 40. And only with the Jukes did they become synonymous with soul music and rhythm and blues, which is what all bar bands are considered to be now — their standard format. That wasn't the case before the Jukes."

By the time Van Zandt joined Springsteen's E Street Band in 1975, John Lyon had put together Southside Johnny & the Asbury Jukes, and was playing as the house band at the Stone Pony in Asbury Park, New Jersey, the famous music venue where Springsteen got his start.

John Lyon and Van Zandt had known each other from playing in various bands together in the early 1970s and had developed a friendship. Even though Van Zandt had joined the E Street Band, he and Lyon were looking to collaborate and create something new — a sound that combined rock and soul music. The result was the Jukes' 1976 debut album, *I Don't Want to Go Home,* an attempt to create and capture that sound.

"Bruce writes a lot of different kinds of songs. And the Jukes' sound had already been established in its live performances, so Bruce thought he had a couple of

214

songs that were appropriate for that particular sound," said Van Zandt.

"At one point, it was very important to Bruce to establish his own sound and his own genre, if you will, which was very much an Americana genre," he said. "And so he would play around with British Invasion stuff, he'd play around with soul music, he'd play around with many different things because he's incredibly versatile as a songwriter."

But Springsteen wasn't interested in doing those songs himself. It wasn't until Springsteen's fifth studio album, *The River* in 1980, that he started to integrate his own tastes and influences into his music and his albums, according to Van Zandt.

"Up to then, most of the songs would end up as outtakes. Instead of letting them just lie on the cutting room floor, he gave a couple of songs to Southside Johnny," said Van Zandt.

Two of those songs, "The Fever" and "You Mean So Much to Me," ended up on *I Don't Want to Go Home*.

Van Zandt was the producer of that album, wrote the title track "I Don't Want to Go Home" as well as two others — "How Come You Treat Me So Bad" and "Sweeter than Honey" — played guitar, and provided vocals on yet another track, "Broke Down Piece of Man."

"The first album was a little more traditional, I would say. We were trying to outline what the group was going to be," said Van Zandt. "It was a bit of an evolution in public. Effective and very popular, but it didn't quite come together until the title track of *This Time It's for Real*. And then we finally made the complete integration for the third album, *Hearts of Stone*."

And that worked out quite well, Van Zandt said.

"It really did help to integrate the 'Jersey Shore Sound' and at the time, really start to flesh out that sound.

When there is more than one artist working, it starts to make the whole context more interesting.

"What we had with Southside, I really didn't appreciate it until later when someone explained to me how we had redefined the entire bar band definition and sound," said Van Zandt. "And then I started to feel good with *Hearts of Stone*, but I needed to move on from there, so I never pursued it. We finally took it back up 15 years later with *Better Days*. And that record, I believe, probably ended up being our best. I think I'm most proud of the fourth album I did with the Jukes."

Those early days as a producer would serve Van Zandt well throughout his musical career, and would eventually bring him right back to the band that influenced him the most – the Rascals.

"I've been good at producing live shows for a long time. It's one of my interests, because I've always felt that's where the rubber meets the road as far as rock and roll goes," said Van Zandt. "Usually we're catching up to the live shows, both in the case of Southside Johnny and in the case of Bruce Springsteen. It wasn't until I started doing my own solo records where the two things came together a little bit. But basically, I was very much a live show producer."

So it wasn't a stretch for Van Zandt – more than 40 years after The Rascals broke up in 1970 – to produce a Broadway-like show that told the story of The Rascals, incorporating a concert into a multimedia show that included video storytelling and top-notch lighting.

In 1997, The Rascals were inducted into the Rock and Roll Hall of Fame. Van Zandt gave the induction speech, and the original Rascals appeared together for the first time in decades and played a few songs.

In 2010, The Rascals reunited for a benefit in New York, and were joined onstage by Van Zandt and

216

Springsteen for a performance of the band's 1966 No. 1 hit, "Good Lovin'."

"It was the first rock band I ever saw, and it had an enormous impact on me, to this day," said Van Zandt. "You can trace the E Street band directly back to The Rascals."

Great moments
in laundry room history

Waking and Dreaming
Orleans

Sometimes, political protesters are paying attention to more than just political issues. Sometimes, they're listening closely to music.

After years of success with the band Orleans and as a solo artist, John Hall decided to put down his guitar and serve the public in a different way. He ran, and won, a seat as a U.S. representative for New York's 19th Congressional District, and served from 2007 through 2011.

Around the middle of his term, Hall realized how much of an impression his music had made on a portion of the citizenry.

There were always protesters waiting outside the Capitol in Washington, D.C. They were there every day rain or shine, snow, sleet, or hail. Sometimes there we' 100 protesters, sometimes there were five.

"But there was this one guy who was there ? time," said Hall. "He looks like he sleeps under a ↓ he wears an old fatigues jacket and jeans that ha' washed, and looks like he never washes his ha' a big imposing guy with a cardboard sign tha' on with a Sharpie, something like 'Presiden' Amendment,' or whatever. It changed eve' was obscure. You could never really tell or what he was against. But I never spoke to him; I just walked by him on the way to vote."

One day Hall was coming down the steps of the Capitol after a series of votes and heard a voice say, "Congressman Hall!" The lawmaker turned around and said, "Yes?" It was the protester that Hall saw on the Capitol steps every day.

The protester walked toward Hall to say something. The Chief of Staff for New York Congressman Eliot Engel saw Hall being approached and came closer. It was around the time that elected officials were preparing to vote on President Barack Obama's healthcare reform bill. Temperatures were running high because of strong opposition to the proposed bill from the Tea Party. Consequently, there was an awareness of safety issues for elected officials and their staff members.

"So here is this big guy, this Chief of Staff for Congressman Engel; he thought I might need help, so he came over to stand next to me while I was talking to this protester," said Hall.

"And the protester leans in and says, 'I've got a message for you.' I said, 'Well, you always have a message.' And he said, 'Thank you,' and I said, 'You're welcome.' And then he said, 'I just wanted to tell you, I really love your rhythm guitar part on 'Spring Fever.' I just about fell over.

"I thought he was going to say, 'Impeach the president!' or 'Stop the healthcare bill!' or 'Stop the war!' It wasn't about one of our hits; it was about another album track. And it wasn't about a lead guitar part; it was about a rhythm guitar part. The guy was really listening," said Hall.

"So you never know. We were in our 20s when we arted making these records and we didn't think cessarily that we'd still be alive now and touring, let ne that people would want to come and hear these

The Vinyl Dialogues

songs. But somehow they permeated the culture to the point where even a protester standing outside the Capitol would know a rhythm guitar part on an obscure track on the *Waking and Dreaming* album."

Orleans — originally formed in 1972 by Hall, Larry Hoppen, Wells Kelly, and Lance Hoppen — was coming off some success with its third album, *Let There Be Music*, in 1975. The album featured the band's highest charting single to that point, "Dance with Me," which peaked at No. 6 on the Billboard Singles Chart.

Let There Be Music, produced by Chuck Plotkin, was the first album that Orleans had made for David Geffen's Asylum Records, which at the time, had The Eagles, Jackson Browne, and Joni Mitchell in its stable of artists.

"It was a very small and very talented group of musicians. And we were keenly aware of the fact that we were being listened to alongside these other acts," said Hall.

After "Dance with Me" became a hit off the *Let There Be Music* album, Orleans was anxious to make the next album, *Waking and Dreaming*, set for release in 1976. The band added drummer Jerry Marotta to the group for the album.

"We wanted to make a record that would make not only the record company executives and promotion men sit up and pay attention, but we were thinking if Don Henley or Glenn Frey happened to hear the music, that they would go, 'Whoa. Those guys really put some work into that and they really nailed it.'"

The track "Waking and Dreaming" epitomized the work ethic and the different influences of the band members at the time, according to Hall.

"The record has a long and sort of unusual format. It builds through a series of chord changes that are unusual so that the music is as close to a funk track as

221

white guys from upstate New York were going to get," said Hall.

"And it was not easy to play and sing at the same time. It was one thing to put down. It was a danceable and interesting bass and guitar in unison. It was hard enough to do in the studio and get it right all the way through. But then when we had to prepare the song for live performances, we found out how hard it really was. But we were just really working seriously at our craft," he said.

Hall and his wife, Johanna, were the songwriters on eight of the ten songs for *Waking and Dreaming*. By that time, the duo had already gained some momentum as songwriters.

Johanna Hall was a music critic and reviewer in the late 1960s and early 1970s for the *Village Voice*, a weekly newspaper in New York City. She and John were just kids in their late teens/early 20s, living together. Johanna had written a positive review of a Janis Joplin record that got Joplin's attention.

"Her publicist called me and said, 'Janis wants to meet you.' And so I went and I met Janis and we became great friends," said Johanna.

"John was like 18 years old at the time and he loved The Beatles and Jimi Hendrix and he was writing catchy music, but his lyrics were written by an 18-year-old boy," she said.

"Janis used to come to our Lower East Side apartment and hang out with us when she was in town. And John would play her some songs," said Johanna. "I guess he was playing her a song one time and as she was leaving, she said, 'You know, why don't the two of you write me a song?' And she looked at me and she said, 'You're a woman, you're a writer, write me a song.' And it was like a command performance for the Queen. She was my fairy godmother. Poof, you're a songwriter."

The Halls wrote the song "Half Moon" and it appeared on Joplin's 1971 album *Pearl*, released after Joplin's death. The single was the B side of "Me and Bobby McGee."

So when it came time for Orleans to cut the album *Waking and Dreaming*, the Halls — who had established themselves as songwriters not only with "Half Moon," but also "Dance with Me" — had several other songs that were ready to go on an album.

One of those songs was "Still the One," which would be the group's highest-charting single in its history, reaching No. 5 on the Billboard charts in 1976.

Johanna Hall wrote the lyrics to that song while doing the laundry.

"I had a friend who said to me, 'Everyone writes songs about breaking up. Why don't you write a song about staying together?' And I thought that was a good idea," said Johanna.

"I can remember doing the laundry and the idea coming to me. I'm sure it's a pretty common thing, when you're doing something else that's more mechanical or physical, like washing the dishes or doing the laundry, anything like that, that your mind is free," she said.

"I do specifically remember I had been mulling over this idea about staying together. And I was doing laundry — that's probably where I grabbed an envelope and started scribbling down ideas and gave them to John.

"He thought it was good. We had a very good writing relationship, always. But I don't think either of us thought that this was going to be the biggest song of our career. We just thought it was going to be a good song."

Johanna admitted that as a songwriter, she was never really one hundred percent satisfied with her work.

"That's because you know where the seams are and you know where you settled and could have done better. There are very few songs, only two or three, that I didn't think, 'Oh, that could be better,'" she said.

As for "Still the One," there are some aspects she liked about it better than others.

"I'm very proud of the lyrics. And in particular, something that maybe doesn't get so noticed — the verses are really good. I'm proud of those verses," she said.

"I'm not as sure about the lyric of the bridge: 'Changing, our love is going gold, even though we grow old, it grows new.' Eh; that's OK. Certainly the chorus is clever — 'scratch my itch,' 'dream about/make me shout,' 'love to touch' — all of those things are really good."

Other songs on *Waking and Dreaming*, in hindsight, may have fallen a little short for one of the album's main songwriters.

"I think some of the songs on that record are a little weak. 'The Burn' is a great song because it's Wells [written by Wells Kelly] and I miss him very much [Kelly died in 1984 after a night of partying while on tour with Meat Loaf]. I think 'Golden State' isn't the greatest song we've ever written, but it was about an infatuation with California. 'The Path' isn't as good a song as it could be," said Johanna. "I think maybe going into that record — it's so long ago — maybe it would have been better if we had a little more time to write more."

Johanna conceived the concept of *Waking and Dreaming* because she was always intrigued by the different worlds of sleeping and waking, and how they both seem so real.

"I would have liked to have carried that through a little more, maybe other than just the song 'Waking and Dreaming.' I think it was a good attempt at something, but I'm not sure it entirely succeeded," she said.

The cover of the *Waking and Dreaming* album features the band members shirtless, all with their eyes open except for John, whose eyes are closed.

"We stood for two hours on a piece of tape while the photographer snapped roll after roll of film and then at the end he said, 'Well, I've got a couple of frames left, why don't you all take your shirts off.' We were just like leaning on each other," said John. "That was his method of getting us in the frame and getting us all to try and interact by getting us all to stand on this piece of tape on the floor."

Johanna's recollection of the cover shoot was slightly different.

"The reason they have no shirts on is because they showed up in ugly shirts," she said. "Not John, I was always buying him a new shirt or something. So John probably looked fine, but the other guys had on horrible things. That's one of the wife's functions: You buy nice shirts for your husband and he looks great. But Larry and Lance in particular didn't have very good taste [in clothes]."

The other unique aspect of the cover was that it was "photo swapped." In the days before Photoshop, pictures were altered by the old cut-and-paste method.

"My head was photo swapped," said John. "The photographer asked us to do one with all of our eyes closed and one with all of our eyes open. The one that was used was the shot with everybody's eyes open. But they took my head from the other shot, where my eyes are closed, which makes it look like I'm looking down. And they imposed that version of my head on the picture. So it's actually two pictures merged together."

"It's acknowledged to be among the worst album covers of all time," said Johanna.

After 30 years of marriage, John and Johanna Hall divorced in 2000. They have a daughter in her mid-30s, but Johanna said that the catalog of songs she and John wrote together are also like their children.

"Still the One" is one of the most recognizable songs from the '70s and has been used as a jingle by ABC television, in television commercials for Burger King, and by President George W. Bush during his 2004 presidential campaign. As a liberal environmentalist Democrat, John Hall didn't appreciate that too much, and since the campaign didn't have Hall's permission to use the song, it was forced to drop it from the campaign playlist after Hall complained.

But the Halls were especially on their game in the mid-1970s, when *Waking and Dreaming* was released.

"Of course, with the success of 'Dance with Me,' that put more pressure on [*Waking and Dreaming*]," said Johanna. "I think that John and I really were at the height of our songwriting abilities and it was just pure joy to be writing songs and to have a great band and a great record company and a great producer who really understood and spoke so intelligently and intuitively about the music."

"The songs have not only been around as songs, but they've been used in movies, they've been used in commercials, they've been used in politics," said John. "Both 'Dance with Me' and 'Still the One' have been used in multiple commercials and are kind of the wallpaper now.

"In the elevator, I hear people — who I don't know — singing or humming along or singing a verse to one of them if it's on in the background," he said. "You know a song has reached a certain level of success when you hear it in the dentist's office. We're very fortunate to have hooked a couple of big fish in the song department."

Capturing lightning in a bottle

Self-titled
Player

ey, nobody's perfect. Back in the 1970s, even legendary record producer and music industry executive Clive Davis occasionally missed one.

Peter Beckett, J.C. Crowley, Ronn Moss, and John Friesen — calling themselves Player — had a handful of songs, maybe four or five, that Beckett and Crowley had written. In 1976 the band's manager set up appointments around Los Angeles with various record label executives and producers to play the songs live, using just acoustic guitars and harmonies.

And a ton of those executives and producers passed on Player, including the already famous Clive Davis, who had been president of Columbia Records from 1967 through 1973. During his tenure there, he signed the likes of Simon & Garfunkel, The Byrds, Bruce Springsteen, Billy Joel, Chicago, Janis Joplin, and Blood, Sweat and Tears, among others.

After leaving Columbia Records, Davis founded Arista Records. As president from 1975 through 2000, he signed many notable artists including Barry Manilow, Aretha Franklin, Carly Simon, and The Grateful Dead.

By 1976, Clive Davis was a pretty big deal. And Player had secured an audience with him in hopes of landing its big break.

"We were at the Beverly Hills Hotel, in the ballroom, and there was nobody in there but Clive," said

Beckett. "We were on stage with no mics, just the acoustic guitars, and he was sitting right in front of the stage in a suit and tie, with his legs crossed.

"By this stage of the game, we had written the single 'Baby Come Back.' We did two songs and then we did 'Baby Come Back,'" said Beckett.

When the band was done playing, Davis gave his immediate and honest assessment.

"After the song, he said, 'You know, you guys look great and you sound wonderful, but I just don't hear a hit,'" said Beckett.

And then Davis proceeded to play some songs by other artists that he thought were hits, as if to show the members of Player what he thought a hit song sounded like.

"To me, they were kind of obscure and I've never heard them since," said Beckett.

After the experience with Davis, Beckett and his bandmates kind of lost faith in themselves — until they got an audience with Dennis Lambert and Brian Potter.

Lambert and Potter were songwriters who had penned tunes for The Grass Roots, and Hamilton, Joe Frank & Reynolds in the late 1960s. By the mid-1970s, they had established their own record label called Haven Records. Their roster included Glen Campbell, Dusty Springfield, The Four Tops, and The Righteous Brothers.

"They had everything going on at the time," said Beckett. "And we played them our songs. When we played 'Baby Come Back,' they both just kind of stopped — with their mouths open — and said, 'This is a hit.' They heard a hit. And they got us in touch with RSO Records and that was it."

RSO — the Robert Stigwood Organization — managed the careers of several big names at the time, including the Bee Gees and Eric Clapton. Player was asked to do another live performance for RSO executives.

"I was pretty cocky in those days and by then we had worked 'Baby Come Back' up with the live band," said Beckett. "And all these guys were sitting in the back of the studio and we did a few songs.

"Then I remember walking up to the mic and saying, 'And now we'd like to do our first No. 1 hit.' And we really belted it out and it felt powerful at the time. It felt like something could happen here. And that was the clincher. We were signed with RSO," said Beckett.

Crowley and Beckett were the songwriters in the band, and now they had an album to write. They already had "Baby Come Back," but only four other songs.

Beckett had met Crowley at a party in Hollywood. Crowley was from Texas and Beckett described him as "an oddball guy," and that was reflected in Crowley's songwriting.

"He had odd little lyrics and he loved The Doobie Brothers," said Beckett. "The Doobies were his favorite band. So he injected a little bit of that into the album. And a little bit of Steely Dan.

"When people critique that album today, they say it sounds like a little bit of Hall & Oates, Steely Dan, and The Doobie Brothers. And that's pretty much what the influences were, I'm sure," he said.

Their eponymous debut album *Player* was released in October 1977. The single "Baby Come Back," co-written by Beckett and Crowley, was a No. 1 hit and stayed on the Billboard chart for a total of 32 weeks.

A second single from the album, "This Time I'm In It for Love," written by Larry Keith and Steve Pippin, reached No. 10 and stayed on the charts for 17 weeks.

When "Baby Come Back" was making its way to the top of the singles chart, RSO put the band on the *Silk Degrees* tour opening for Boz Scaggs, where it was playing 30,000-seat arenas.

Silk Degrees was the seventh studio album for Boz Scaggs and featured three Top 40 hits: "It's Over," "Lowdown," and "Lido Shuffle." The album reached No. 2 on the charts and spent 115 weeks on the Billboard Top 200 albums.

After the Scaggs tour — and because Clapton was on the same label as Player — RSO had the band open for Clapton on his *Slowhand* tour, which was in support of his fifth studio album, released in 1977.

"We didn't know it was going to be such a famous tour, probably Clapton's most famous ever," said Beckett. "And we thought, 'Oh my God, it's Eric Clapton!'"

"Strangely enough, we've had five or six charting singles and truthfully, most people don't know us for anything other than 'Baby Come Back.' But 'This Time I'm In It for Love" was a No. 10 song, which is a pretty huge hit, and it's barely known. But everybody knows 'Baby Come Back.' Everything else got overshadowed by that," said Beckett.

After four albums, Player disbanded.

Moss went on in 1987 to become a television star playing fashion mogul Ridge Forrester in the daytime soap opera, *The Bold and the Beautiful.*

Beckett started writing songs for artists like Olivia Newton-John, Kenny Rogers, and The Temptations. He also wrote songs for film and television before joining Little River Band in 1989. He toured with that group for nearly a decade.

"I would have liked to have had more hits," said Beckett. "Luckily I've written for other people and I've had a lot of movie and TV stuff, so I'm doing OK.

"But I'm grateful for capturing lightning in a bottle. You're very, very lucky if you get anything that even smells of a hit," he said. "And you're really lucky to get a No. 1 hit. And you're extremely lucky to get anything more than that. And I've been lucky enough to get a little more than that, so you know, I'm grateful. I really am."

Beckett said that naturally things have aged and production styles have changed over the decades, but he believes the *Player* album still sounds pretty good.

"I'll give you an example. I think my best work personally was my solo album in 1991," he said of his first solo album, *Beckett,* on the Curb label.

"I think the songwriting is really good and some of my favorite songs are on that album, some of them that we actually still do on stage today.

"I loved it at the time. It was the early '90s and everything was just awash with reverb — huge drums and big echoes on vocals and everything," said Beckett. "And today, I love the songs but I can't listen to it because of the reverb.

"Being a producer, I just can't stand too much reverb. But when I listen to the early Player stuff, there's hardly any reverb on it. It's real dry, and I think those are the sounds and songs that stand the test of time," he said. "When you get into too much of a stylized age, the songs age really easy. So in one way, I prefer my solo album. But production-wise, I prefer the first Player album."

Moss and Beckett still tour today as Player. They appeared in 2013 with other artists from the 1970s — Christopher Cross, Orleans, John Ford Coley, and Firefall — in soft rock tours.

"Every song on these tours is a hit," said Beckett. "You're only on stage for 15 minutes. You do your hits and that's pretty much it. You want to play for another hour or two, but it's just the way it is."

And still, it all comes back around to "Baby Come Back," more than 35 years after the song's release. And Beckett's OK with that.

"Most of the stories I hear from people about 'Baby Come Back' are unfit to relate," he said with a smile. "It usually has something to do with the back seat of a car and I lost this to that. Enough said."

Everybody's got a 'Groove Thing'

2 Hot!
Peaches and Herb

As a teenager just out of high school, Herb Feemster used to love hanging around the historic Howard Theatre in Washington, D.C.

In its heyday, the theater hosted many of the great "colored" artists of the 1950s and 1960s, including Sammy Davis, Jr., James Brown, Little Stevie Wonder, The Supremes, Dionne Warwick, Lionel Hampton, and Lena Horne.

Feemster wanted to get into the music industry, so in 1964 he got a job as a salesman at Waxie Maxie's Quality Music Shop, a chain of record stores with one shop just around the corner from the Howard Theatre. While working at Waxie Maxie's, he met a couple of guys, Freddie Perren and Van McCoy, who were also looking to get into the music industry.

And the Howard Theatre offered the opportunity to meet musicians and record producers.

Per their dreams, all three would end up in the music industry.

Feemster became Herb Fame of the singing duo Peaches and Herb; McCoy became a successful singer, songwriter, and producer for such artists as Gladys Knight and the Pips, Aretha Franklin, and The Stylistics; and Perren became a songwriter and producer who had worked in Motown for Berry Gordy's group of

233

songwriters and record producers known collectively as
"The Corporation."

Fame and McCoy's paths crossed again in 1966
when McCoy, then a record producer for Columbia
Records, signed Fame and Francine "Peaches" Barker to
Columbia subsidiary Date Records, as Peaches and Herb.
The duo had some success with singles and albums for the
next couple of years, but touring became too much for
Barker. Although Barker continued to record with Fame
on all in-studio Date Records recording projects, she was
replaced on stage during tours by a "second" Peaches,
Marlene Mack.

Fame retired from the act in 1970 in order to
pursue a career in law enforcement, eventually landing a
job with the Washington, D.C. Police Department. But
after six years in law enforcement, Fame decided to get
back into the music business.

Once again, he turned to McCoy, who introduced
him to Linda Greene, the third "Peaches" in the Peaches
and Herb duo. There would eventually be six "Peaches"
throughout the Peaches and Herb act. Together, they
recorded their first album for MCA Records — the
eponymous *Peaches and Herb* in 1977 — produced by
McCoy.

That first album failed to chart. A year later, Fame
and Greene were in New York City and ran into Perren,
who was starting his own label — MVP/Polydor — and
who wanted to sign Peaches and Herb.

Fame and Greene agreed to join Perren and left
McCoy. On the strength of two singles — "Shake Your
Groove Thing" and "Reunited" — the duo made the *2
Hot!* album for MVP/Polydor in 1978, and it became the
most successful album ever for Peaches and Herb.

"The album was basically Freddie Perren's
concept," said Fame. "What Freddie and Dino [Fekaris, a
songwriter] did was that they would pick songs, play them

for us, and see if we wanted to do them. Every song that we recorded, there was always a period where they would say, 'Should we do it this way or is it better another way?' And then we'd make a decision, which was the right way. It was never, never, never a dictatorship.

"And we wanted to do a song that ordinarily people wouldn't think Peaches and Herb would do. And that song was 'Shake Your Groove Thing.'"

"Shake Your Groove Thing," written by Perren and Fekaris, reached No. 2 on the Billboard charts in 1978.

"No one expected that from us because everything we had done in the past was about love, love, love, love, love," said Fame. "That was our image, anyway. But it was the disco era and I knew we had that disco flavor.

"Every artist that goes in wants to do something that's great or that will last forever. And 'Shake Your Groove Thing' was new for me because I had never done anything like that."

Fame said that the disco era kind of surprised him when it burst into the public consciousness in the mid-1970s. But he liked the music because he liked to, well, shake his groove thing.

"I loved to dance. We danced all the time here in D.C. If you couldn't dance and you were from D.C., you'd better go hide someplace," said Fame.

"But the disco era was like a great giant of music that made people get up and want to dance," he said. "You couldn't sit in your seat. There was so much music out there that made you tap your feet and then get up and dance."

Fame said at first, "Shake Your Groove Thing" was just a disco song that he enjoyed, but he didn't predict it would hit as big as it did.

"Everybody has a groove thing," said Fame. "It could be shaking your finger, it could be shaking your head, it could be just walking and clapping. You know what your groove thing is and you work it. And the disco era was like a big, huge, humongous dance craze."

Although the success of "Shake Your Groove Thing" may have caught Fame off guard, the second single from *2 Hot!* was a big deal right from the get-go, and everyone involved seemed to know it.

"There is only one song that I knew was going to be a hit for us, and that was 'Reunited,'" said Fame. "When it was first played for us on the piano by Freddie and Dino, for some reason, Linda started crying. And we said, 'Whoa, what's up with that?' It was like, 'This is going to be a big song.' And fortunately, it was.

"She felt it right from the beginning," said Fame. "You know I wasn't gonna stand up there and cry."

Fame said that there was initial concern with "Shake Your Groove Thing" and "Reunited," because both singles nearly got in each other's way when it came to radio air time.

When the record company shipped "Shake Your Groove Thing" to the radio stations, "Reunited" was on the flip side.

"And that was a mistake because the disc jockeys wanted to play 'Reunited' right away, but the record company had to hold them off of playing it until 'Shake Your Groove Thing' had run its course," said Fame.

"Reunited" was a crossover smash hit, topping both the pop and soul charts, and was eventually nominated for a Grammy in the "Song of the Year" category nearly two years after its release.

As successful as those two singles made the *2 Hot!* album, Fame said — more than 35 years after the album's release — that he thought there should have been a third single released from that album: "Four's a Traffic Jam."

236

The song is about falling out of love with one's spouse and falling in love with another. But Fame didn't push for it to be another single.

"I loved that song, but I didn't express my opinion about it at the time," said Fame. "I liked everything about it — the way it started, what we said, how it was put together.

"I just thought it was a song [about what] a lot of people go through every day. It's what happens in life. People fall in love and they get married and somewhere along the line, they fall out of love with their spouses and fall in love with someone else. And then they realize, 'We can't do this because we have children.' It happens every day," said Fame.

"I can tell you now that I should have said something, but I didn't. And I know why," he said. "I'm an inside person. I keep most things inside, I solve my problems myself; I don't include other people. That's part of me. It's just that I didn't say anything. And I should have, but I didn't."

One of the reasons that Fame and Greene were successful with *2 Hot!* was that they genuinely liked each other.

"We could go out and have coffee. I just liked her," said Fame. "She's always been a sweet kind of person, just a nice lady. And it worked and it showed. When we worked together or separately in the studio, we were always eager to get it done. We just enjoyed being in the studio together and out of the studio together."

Of course, if a duo is going to make an album called *2 Hot!* then the album cover ought to reflect that certain hotness. And the *2 Hot!* album cover doesn't disappoint. But hold on a minute; it's not really what it looks like.

The cover features Peaches and Herb, noses touching, staring longingly into each other's eyes, with

Peaches' left hand on Herb's chest . . . and with a little creative photo editing, it looks like Peaches' hand is producing some red-hot heat onto Herb's chest. It is, well . . . too hot.

"It's just like acting; you have to act the part," said Fame. "We liked each other and we enjoyed each other, but I've always been married. So it's just an acting job, that's all. After they take 500 photos at a photo shoot, they ought to get one they can use on the cover."

Fame said his impression now, more than 35 years after its release, is that the album *2 Hot!* was "done in love, and it shows."

"I still play it and I still listen for things I could have done differently after all these years," he said. "Every artist has in mind when they record to create something that will last. I feel — and I'm going to use the right word here — that we have been blessed to have done that.

"My family says that I don't realize the magnitude of what I've done, and I guess I don't. But I'm just happy that it happened because that's what I wanted as a kid. Not too many people get to do in life what they want to do. It happened for me – that's my blessing and that's what I enjoy.

"I still want people to be quiet when I'm in the house or in the car and I hear something by Peaches and Herb. I want to listen; I want to hear it," he said. "I just turn it up. Sometimes, I sing along with my own songs. I have to tell myself to shut up."

Throughout the disco era and the success that Peaches and Herb had in the late 1970s, Fame said he has only one regret: not getting another chance to record with famed Philadelphia record producers Kenny Gamble and Leon Huff.

Fame and the original Peaches — Francine Hurd Barker — had recorded a song called "United" in the late

238

1960s with Gamble and Huff. But that was the only time that Fame got to work with the legendary producers.

"For years I wanted to record again with them, but they would never do it," said Fame. "There was some friction at the time between Gamble and Huff and our manager, David Kapralik, who managed us and Sly and the Family Stone. Even after we parted company with David, they would never use us.

"My whole body wanted to record with them again. I even took a couple of trips up to Philly to see them. But they never gave me a reason why and I always wondered," said Fame.

Still, Fame said there wasn't anything quite like having the success with records and appearing on television shows like Dick Clark's *American Bandstand* and *Soul Train,* created, produced, and hosted by Don Cornelius.

"On *Soul Train* or *American Bandstand,* you'd just look out there and see those kids groovin' to what you've created and that's got to be a mind-blower for anybody," said Fame. "Anybody who tells you different . . . that's bull. It was just outstanding."

From tragedy to triumph

Hot Streets
Chicago

C hicago was looking to rise from the ashes after a tragedy. And the band's 12th album, *Hot Streets*, released in 1978, provided the group with that opportunity.

On January 23, 1978, guitarist and Chicago co-founder Terry Kath, a gun enthusiast, died of a self-inflicted gunshot wound. News accounts reported that Kath and his wife had been drinking at the home of a friend, and Kath put what he thought was an unloaded pistol to his head and pulled the trigger.

According to the Associated Press, police officials reported that Kath said to his wife and friends, "Don't worry, it's not loaded."

It was loaded. Kath died instantly.

When it was time for Chicago to get back into the studio, the loss of its guitarist was still fresh in the minds of band members Peter Cetera, Laudir de Oliveira, Robert Lamm, Lee Loughnane, James Pankow, Walter Parazaider, and Danny Seraphine.

"We were reeling from Terry's death," said drummer Seraphine.

And though the band had to find a new guitarist to replace Kath, there was hope for what the future might hold, musically.

"His replacement was Donnie Dacus and it was working really, really good," said Seraphine.

Dacus had worked with Stephen Stills and Roger McGuinn before accepting the offer to join Chicago.

"The future, after going through such a tragedy and losing Terry like that, once again felt bright. Everyone was rooting for us and it just was a completely uplifting experience," said Seraphine.

So they made changes. *Hot Streets* would be Chicago's first record of all new material since the release of its second album, *Chicago*, in 1970.

And there were more changes. Chicago parted ways with longtime producer James William Guercio, who had been with the band since its inception, and turned to legendary producer Phil Ramone for *Hot Streets*.

"The relationship had gone bad [with Guercio]. If you listen to the body of work we did with him, it's the best. But everybody we worked with, I felt, we did great records with. Phil Ramone was one of them," said Seraphine.

"And working with Phil, as opposed to working with Jimmy, their styles were different. Plus, we had a great, great relationship with Phil. And if you knew him, he was an absolute wonderful person to work with. He got things out of you positively. He always used positive reinforcement. He wasn't heavy handed in the studio at all. If he had to be, he would, but he didn't have to be with us. So there was a great deal of respect between us."

After years of recording albums at Guercio's Caribou Ranch in Colorado, *Hot Streets* was recorded in Los Angeles and at Criteria Studios in Miami. The Miami location provided the band with an unexpected opportunity for collaboration, because it put them in the same studio as the Bee Gees. And in 1978, the Bee Gees were hot.

They were just coming off the mega-hit *Saturday Night Fever* soundtrack album released in November of 1977, and were back at Criteria Studios cutting their 15th album, *Spirits Have Flown*.

Getting the Bees Gees to add vocals to *Hot Streets* was as easy as walking to the next door in the studio and asking them.

"We got to know each other and we became friends and started talking about collaborating," said Seraphine. "We [the horn section of Pankow, Parazaider and Loughnane] played on one of their tracks and they [the Bee Gees] sang on 'Little Miss Lovin',' a song that Peter [Cetera] wrote. It was really cool."

Bee Gees keyboardist Blue Weaver also contributed on the song "No Tell Lover," written by Cetera, Loughnane, and Seraphine.

"'No Tell Lover' should have been a Top 5 record, but there were other records — big, big hits — that didn't move down the chart and that's why 'No Tell Lover' didn't move into the Top 10, and ultimately the Top 5. And it should have. It's Top 15, so it's still considered a hit," said Seraphine.

And there are a lot of other great songs on the album as well, Seraphine said.

"Robert [Lamm] wrote some really great songs. 'Hot Streets' itself is just really a cool song. That's musically a very challenging song and I have some songs on there that I think were some of the best I ever wrote," said Seraphine, who has writing credits for "The Greatest Love on Earth," "Ain't It Time," "No Tell Lover," and "Show Me the Way" on the album.

"On 'The Greatest Love on Earth,' Billy Joel was working with Phil at the time, and he told Phil he thought that was a smash hit. It never was released [as a single], but that's a really good song," said Seraphine.

243

Upon its release *Hot Streets* did well, peaking at No. 12 on the charts and eventually going platinum. But it didn't get the respect that Seraphine thought it should have received.

"It didn't, for some reason. It sold like a million and a half units, but the record company was expecting more and wanted more. And they [record company officials] weren't happy with it," said Seraphine. "I couldn't begin to know why. Timing maybe? I don't know what happened. We did one more album with Phil and then we moved on."

In addition to the new material, the album also had a new cover, which deviated from what fans had come to expect throughout the decade from Chicago album covers. Starting with the 1971 album *Chicago III* and continuing to the 1977 album *Chicago XI*, the band's album covers simply featured the name of the band and the Roman numeral reflecting the number of the album.

The *Hot Streets* album cover art is markedly different from that formula. It features the band members in casual, fun-loving, and even somewhat goofy shots. For example, Seraphine is shown in the arms of Cetera, both embraced in a big hug and sporting big grins.

"I'm in the hat and I'm straddling Peter," said Seraphine. "That looks a little perverted now. It was just kind of a fun thing between me and Peter. That was a Norman Seeff [the photographer] thing; he liked those kinds of pictures.

"I think we're all in the same shot. Norman might have stripped different guys out and put them in different positions to make a composite, but I remember doing it all together. I think it was a real cut-and-paste thing, where they actually cut it and pasted. It's amazing the way they did those covers in those days without the technology that we have today," said Seraphine.

"We were just screwing around trying to give Norman what he wanted. I think he wanted animation."

Throughout the years, Seraphine has remained proud of *Hot Streets*.

"It was a great album and it was a great feeling to rise from the ashes, so to speak, once again," he said. "*Hot Streets* holds a place really near and dear in my heart, and I'm pretty sure that everybody else in the band would say the same thing. *Hot Streets* was a really defining moment and a really good record."

'The Geator with the Heator' analyzes the decade

Epilogue
Jerry Blavat

S ome things have never changed for Jerry Blavat. When rock and roll was beginning to evolve from rhythm and blues, it was the beat, man, that appealed to the kid from South Philly, and stayed with him forever.

In the early years of *American Bandstand* — known just as *Bandstand* from 1952 to 1957 — Blavat was one of the show's teenage dancers.

"I'm a dancer; I hear the rhythm and beat and it touches my soul," said Blavat.

And more than 60 years later, the phrase "It's got a good beat and you can dance to it" — popularized by Dick Clark's *American Bandstand* in the early 1960s during the show's "Rate-a-Record" segment — is still the credo by which Blavat lives.

Blavat would go on to become a Philadelphia icon known as "The Geator with the Heator" and "The Boss with the Hot Sauce." He worked as a radio deejay, television host, record promoter, and nightclub entrepreneur. His familiar sign-off, "Keep on rockin,' cause you only rock once!" carried him all the way to induction into the Rock and Roll Hall of Fame in 1998.

He's had a front-row seat in every era of music beginning in the 1950s, which makes him eminently qualified to analyze the music from the 1970s, particularly the evolution of Philly soul, the Jersey Shore Sound and disco music.

"If it's got a rhythm, if it's got a beat, and you can listen to it and it reaches your ear and touches your heart — you can dance to it, man. I never locked myself into one format. I played music from the heart," said Blavat.

When Dick Clark decided to move *American Bandstand* from Philadelphia to Los Angeles in early 1964, that left a void in Philadelphia. Television producers were looking for a local show to replace *American Bandstand* and they turned to The Geator for help.

Blavat didn't try to reinvent the wheel. He stuck with what he knew and in 1965 built a show that would revolve around the beat — the sound — of the music. It was called *The Discophonic Scene* and it featured teenage dancers and guest artists.

From 1965 to 1968, *The Discophonic Scene* was hot. And by the time the 1970s rolled around, Blavat was well-ingrained into the local, regional, and national music scenes.

The 1970s brought with it the evolution of the Philly soul sound. Music producers Kenny Gamble and Leon Huff formed the Philadelphia International Records label in 1971, which featured such artists as The O'Jays, Harold Melvin and the Blue Notes (with lead singer Teddy Pendergrass), Billy Paul, McFadden and Whitehead, The Three Degrees, and Lou Rawls.

The producers focused on sound and arrangement to develop the genre, which essentially laid the groundwork for what was to become disco music later in the decade.

"I knew exactly where they [Gamble and Huff] were going. The only thing they were doing differently than what they did in the 1960s — when they were producing groups like The Intruders and all that other stuff — was adding big orchestration," said Blavat.

The Intruders were one of the first groups to have hits for Gamble and Huff, and they had a major influence on the development of Philly soul.

"All they did was take rhythm and blues and add a large orchestration to it. And they added lyrics that were part of the time period."

According to Blavat, it came down to just that — taking big orchestration and continuing to develop the beat.

"You take the early things that Big Joe Turner did, like the 'Midnight Special' or 'Shake, Rattle and Roll' or 'Honey Hush;' you take that rhythm and you take Little Richard and Lloyd Price when he did 'Stagger Lee' — that was rock and roll with 22 pieces back then that they carried on the road," said Blavat.

"In the '60s, what happened was Johnny Rivers did 'Maybelline' and it worked with that rhythm beat. You take the song in the '70s with 'Brazil,' which the Ritchie Family did — that song goes back to the '30s. It was a rhythm and beat with orchestration."

By the time disco came around in the mid-to-late-1970s, Blavat had restyled his 1960s show, and *The Discophonic Scene* became *The Discophonic Scene II*.

"It was a takeoff of my show in the '60s, except instead of me playing Otis Redding, instead of me playing Chuck Berry, I played KC and the Sunshine Band. And the younger generation was picking up on that," he said.

Once again — much like it was for Philly soul — disco was the beat with a large orchestration that helped define the sound, according to Blavat.

"A song like 'YMCA' [by The Village People] has lyrics, it's rhythmical, and you can sing along to it," said Blavat.

Radio deejay, television host, record promoter, nightclub entrepreneur and Philadelphia icon Jerry Blavat, second from left, is pictured here in the 1970s with members of The Soul Survivors, a Philadelphia-based R&B group.
(Photo courtesy of Jerry Blavat)

Between the sounds of Philly soul and disco in the mid-1970s, an East Coast sound emerged that had lineage starting with The Rascals and continuing through Bruce Springsteen and Steven Van Zandt, and onto Southside Johnny & the Asbury Jukes.

Springsteen was just becoming Springsteen around that time, and was not only a big fan of rock and roll, but also a fan of The Geator's radio show and his nightclub, "Memories," in Margate, New Jersey.

"He would come to 'Memories' and he would sneak in to see what the kids were doing and what the kids were dancing to. And they were dancing to the stuff in the '70s. This is at the very beginning of his career, even before he hit," said Blavat. "Nobody invented the wheel. It was just the transition to where it was into the '70s."

250

According to Blavat, Springsteen applied the rhythm beat that was happening in the 1970s to Springsteen's "Elvis Presley sound" and "he became a gigantic star by applying his talent to that which was yesterday."

Van Zandt and Southside Johnny (John Lyon) are cut from the same cloth, Blavat said.

"I don't think Southside was doing anything different than Springsteen. I think that maybe Southside Johnny's beat is a little more rock and roll than maybe Springsteen's," he said. "The problem with Southside Johnny is that he did not have the marketing. Everything in this industry is marketing and packaging. There are so many great groups out there who unfortunately don't get the opportunity to be heard, who are just as good as Springsteen or just as good as some of these other groups.

"Springsteen's early inspiration was Elvis. He just took it a step above that. He was hanging out in Asbury Park and Seaside Heights, going into clubs and listening to what was happening," said Blavat.

"Springsteen had the swagger of an old rock and roll star. He could have been a Georgie Burnett, Johnny Burnett, Ronnie Hawkins; these were the cats with the swagger, man, the sound. Listen to Ronnie Hawkins doing 'Mary Lou.' You can get that song today and get an artist of today to do it and it would be a smash. It's all rock and roll."

There's no doubt in Blavat's mind that as the 1960s progressed into the 1970s and beyond, the music just got bigger and bigger. And it got better.

"Whatever the era, I mean even today, if it's got a beat, if it's got a rhythm to it, if it's got a lyric that speaks from one's heart, I'm on it," said Blavat. "Music is universal. Music has no timeframe. If it's good, it's good."

Acknowledgements

Projects like this are a collaborative effort. I'd like to thank so many people for their contributions toward making *The Vinyl Dialogues* a reality.

I must start with my friend, mentor, and editor Frank Quattrone, who offered his endless encouragement and musical expertise; and editors Ruth Littner and Ann Stolinsky of Gemini Wordsmiths (www.geminiwordsmiths.com), whose professionalism and expertise put a shine on the copy.

The eye-catching front and back cover designs are the work of the incredibly talented Ron Dacanay, a longtime friend and colleague.

I enjoyed interviewing the artists in the book and I appreciate their willingness to share their stories with me. I particularly enjoyed the opportunity to collaborate with Doug Clifford of Creedence Clearwater Revival, Bruce Johnston of The Beach Boys, Johanna Hall of Orleans, Dennis Locorriere of Dr. Hook, Don Reid of The Statler Brothers, and legendary Philadelphia icon, Jerry Blavat.

The publicists for the artists played a vital role in setting up the interviews, and none was more important to the project than Jonathan Wolfson of Wolfson Entertainment, the manager for Daryl Hall and John Oates. Jonathan always made the Rock and Roll Hall of Famers available for my interview requests, and Daryl and John have been gracious with their time on many occasions over the years.

Thanks also to publicist Jay Jones who represented The Beach Boys but is now director of media relations for the Country Music Association; Erin

253

Edwards, who represents the band, America; Caroline
Stegner of D. Baron Media Relations, Inc.; Caitlin
DeForest of Webster Public Relations; Robin Pao and U-
Jung Jung of Chapman and Co. Management; Mike
Farley of Michael J. Media Group/<u>Bullz-Eye.com</u>;
Howard Wuelfing of Howlin' Wuelf Media; Alan
Rommelfanger of Daybreak Entertainment; Jason
Engstrom of Entertainment Services International; Dave
Chesler and Emily McGill of Larry Magid Entertainment
Group and the Hartman Group; Jeff Albright of Albright
Entertainment Group; Michelle Kaylan, wife of Howard
Kaylan of Flo & Eddie; Julie Hayles of H2H Consulting,
LLC; Benita Teems of McCain and Co. Public Relations;
Yvette Shearer of Shearer Public Relations; Rose
Nangano, managerial assistant for Roger Earl, and Linda
Arcello-Earl of Noisy S.O.D. Management; and Bruce
Garfield of BGE.

Special thanks go to Carol Tempesta,
administrative assistant, and Keely Stahl, personal
assistant to Jerry Blavat at Geator Gold Radio, for their
help finding appropriate photos to use in this book; to
Larry Cultrera for allowing me to use his photos of the
Abandoned Luncheonette; and to Bob Hammond, whose
idea it was to ask Jerry Blavat to provide an analysis of
the decade.

And finally, to my wife Judy, without whose love
and support this book would not have been possible; and
to my family, the Pennsylvania contingent of daughter
Kiley and son-in-law Mat Shetler, daughter Lexi Morsch,
stepdaughter Kaitie Hughes, stepson Kevin Hughes, and
father-in-law Walt Wiesenhutter; and to the Illinois
contingent that includes my mother, Ann Morsch, sister
Casey Gambetti, and brother Matt Morsch, who are
always there for me.

About the author

Mike Morsch is a 37-year veteran of the newspaper business, having served as a reporter, columnist, and editor at newspapers in Iowa, Illinois, and Pennsylvania.

Mike has earned several awards for his writings from the Illinois Press Association, Suburban Newspapers of America (now the Local Media Association), the Pennsylvania Newspaper Association and the Philadelphia Press Association.

His first book, *Dancing in My Underwear: The Soundtrack of My Life*, was published by Biblio Publishing in 2012.

A 1982 graduate of the University of Iowa, he earned a Bachelor of Science degree in journalism and was a two-year letterman on the Hawkeyes' baseball team.

He is married to Judy, "The Blonde Accountant," and the couple resides in North Wales, Pennsylvania. He has two daughters, Kiley Shetler and Lexi Morsch, and two stepchildren, Kaitie Hughes and Kevin Hughes.

You can contact Mike at msquared35@yahoo.com

INDEX

258

261

R

S

T

CPSIA information can be obtained at www.ICGtesting.com
Printed in the USA
BVOW01s0549290716

457017BV00010B/144/P